Successful Teaching Placement in Scotland

Primary and Early Years

Successful Teaching Placement in Scotland

Primary and Early Years

Jane Medwell and Frances Simpson

Acknowledgements

The documents on pages 126, 128 and 130 are produced by the General Teaching Council for Scotland and are available via the GTCS website www.gtcs.org.uk

First published in 2008 by Learning Matters Ltd.

British Library Cataloguing in Publication Data
A CIP record for this book is available from the British Library.

ISBN 978 1 84445 171 5

Cover design by Code 5 Design Associates Ltd
Project management by Deer Park Productions, Tavistock, Devon
Typeset by PDQ Typesetting Ltd
Printed and bound in Great Britain by Cromwell Press Ltd, Trowbridge, Wiltshire

Learning Matters Ltd
33 Southernhay East
Exeter EX1 1NX
Tel: 01392 215560
info@learningmatters.co.uk
www.learningmatters.co.uk

Contents

Introduction

This book is intended for those who want to teach in Primary and Early Years (3–11).

To become a qualified teacher you need to reach the benchmark Standard for Full Registration. This is achieved in stages, the first of which is to study at one of six Scottish Universities to complete and pass a course of Initial Teacher Education. This allows you to register with the General Teaching Council for Scotland (GTCS) at a provisional level. Full registration can only be achieved upon successful completion of a probationary period (normally one year).

Fully registered teachers are expected 'to be committed to life-long learning and to identify their own professional development needs through a process of self-evaluation and review which allows them to maintain and enhance the Standard for Full Registration.' (Scottish Executive: 2006) As a teacher you are therefore expected to keep reflecting on your work and to keep developing your knowledge and skills throughout your career.

Routes to achieving the Standard for Initial Teacher Education

There are a number of options for study towards the Standard for Initial Teacher Education. All are run by one of six Universities in Scotland – Aberdeen, Dundee, Edinburgh, Glasgow, Paisley or Strathclyde. Stirling University currently only offers training for secondary teachers. All these Universities work together with schools and local authorities to form partnerships that allow for training both within the University and within the school setting.

The route undertaken by the majority of students every year is the Post Graduate Diploma in Education or PGDE. This award is open to those who have successfully completed a degree course of any sort and who have reached required standards of language and maths (see entry requirements for each University). This is usually a one year course and at least half of it (minimum of 18 weeks) will be spent on school or nursery placements where you will develop your teaching skills.

Some universities are now running part-time courses leading to a PGDE. This route takes 21 months and is currently intended for those employed by partner local authorities. Some universities also run courses based well away from the university campus, in particular in the Highlands and Islands and in Dumfries and Galloway. Such arrangements involve students meeting in local colleges for university lectures and workshops (either by visiting lecturers from the main campus or by video-link) and having local mentors who oversee their training. Training is now also available in the Gaelic medium at some universities and centres.

If you have not already obtained a degree, you may undertake an undergraduate degree course to complete your initial teacher education. This will be a four year course leading to a BEd degree with teaching.

The demands of an undergraduate degree are different to those of a PGDE because you also have study challenges to address – you are learning to become a successful learner to degree standard as well as a teacher. You will undertake at least 30 weeks of school or nursery placement during the four years.

These are the routes leading to provisional registration for teaching in Scotland. Following successful completion of ITE, you will then move on to training as a probationary teacher which takes place entirely in school.

This usually consists of a one year placement in a designated school under the Teacher Induction Scheme (TIS) during which you will teach part-time in class and spend the rest of the time on professional development assisted by a mentor and professional development sessions organised by your local authority.

The alternative route is for those not eligible for the TIS, or who decide to opt out of the scheme perhaps from a need to work part-time. This route involves either:

- working as a supply teacher and accumulating the required number of days from short term contracts or part-time contracts;
- working in the independent sector; or
- completing the probationary period outside Scotland.

This route can take up to four terms (270 days) to complete.

This book will be of use to you whichever route you take towards full registration. Chapters 1 to 8 deal with school placements and Chapter 9 covers the probationary period either on the TIS scheme or on supply.

CASE STUDIES

Jane completed her first degree in French and German, travelled abroad for a year, worked for a charity running a play scheme and then began her Primary (5–11) PGDE. She did a placement in P1 of a large city school and a longer placement in P5 of a suburban school. She has just completed her probation year and hopes to develop foreign language teaching in her primary school. Jane found her PGDE 'a really, really, tough year. But a fantastic experience with an incredible learning curve. I wouldn't have wanted any longer because after my long placement I was desperate to have a class of my own. To move the furniture and so on...'

Judy did a degree in biological science and was an environmental health officer for fifteen years. When her children went to secondary school she did a PGDE to re-train as a primary teacher. 'It was very demanding but I was ready for the challenge and the intensity (one year full-time) suited me. I have never regretted it. I found my first placement (in P2) awful but then went into P7 and P5 and loved both. I learnt that each class is very different...' Judy is an IT co-ordinator in a large city school.

Petra did a four-year BEd course. She did short placements in her first and second years in P3 and P7 in two different schools. In her third and fourth years, Petra had a P2 and a P7 placement in the same school. 'I started really slowly. I just had no idea what school was like from the teacher's side. But by my third year I was a totally different person. My knowledge of my subjects has changed out of all recognition and I've matured. I have learned so much and grown as a person on my placements and I feel I have grown into the role of the teacher. My mentors and class teachers were tireless in pushing me but also gave me the confidence I needed.' Petra is now Special Needs co-ordinator in a suburban primary school.

The Standard for Provisional Teacher Registration and professional placements

Whatever route you take through ITE, you will be aiming to demonstrate that you have met the professional standards for initial teacher education known as the Benchmark Standards for ITE. Achieving these standards allows you to apply for provisional registration with the GTCS. The standards will be clearly set out in your course documentation and are also available on the GTCS website. They have three interrelated sections.

1. Professional knowledge and understanding.
2. Professional skills and abilities.
3. Professional values and personal commitment.

You need to know these Standards really well as you will be using them to monitor your progress, set targets and shape your placements. You will have a chance to demonstrate most of the Standards during your professional placements.

Your course will be designed to enable you to demonstrate you have met these standards but the responsibility for collecting the evidence that you have met them is yours. You will be deeply involved in setting your targets, reviewing evidence and monitoring your progress. Your course handbook or guide will suggest formats and processes for doing this and each course is different. This book refers you to your course guidance whenever necessary.

The role of professional placements in ITE

The way each ITE university plans courses will be similar but they involve many similar experiences. As part of your ITE you will experience taught sessions in a university and may have visiting speakers coming to the university to teach you. You will be asked to audit and improve certain aspects of your subject knowledge through self-study. However, all courses have professional placements in schools (including Nurseries) as a central part of their training as a government requirement.

In schools you will be able to observe the way the subject knowledge you are acquiring is used and you will be able to see how teaching techniques are used. You will also learn about the culture and values of schools. These experiences are vital to all trainees. In school you will also be able to practise your planning, teaching and assessing, and the use of the subject knowledge you are developing. In school you will set targets for yourself and the children and assess and monitor your progress with feedback from at least one member of staff. Your mentor will be able to teach, direct and support you in improving your subject knowledge, planning, teaching and assessing – in short, to train you.

This raises a difficulty with terminology. Each university may use its own terminology and your course may use terms such as 'supervised teaching practice', 'school experience', 'serial days', 'school visits', 'professional placement'. We use the term professional placement to identify a period when you are assigned chiefly to a particular class.

During a professional placement you will undertake a number of forms of training:

- observation of particular children, class or group activities, aspects of management or teachers;
- planning;
- teaching and assessing pupils;
- reviewing your progress with feedback from staff;
- undertaking directed tasks;
- learning particular policies and curricula;
- taking part in meetings and in-service sessions.

Many, but not all, of these experiences will be based in one class that you will get to know and teach for a substantial period of time. However, you will have some training needs that may require you to observe or teach in other classes or age phases and you will certainly want to develop your knowledge of progression and continuity through the age ranges. Professional placement is an important part of your training and offers training in all aspects of the Standards. It is important that you do not fall into the trap of thinking that professional placement is only a time to practise what you have learned elsewhere. There are key school staff who will participate in your training in school.

You may also have a *mentor*, a person assigned to oversee your training in school and participate in the assessment of your placement. The mentor will have been trained for his/ her role. Your mentor may, or may not, be the same person as your *class teacher* who will work with you in your class and may participate in observing, advising and assessing you, as well as offering ongoing support. You will also have a *course tutor* (known as 'link tutor', 'adviser', or 'visiting tutor' in different courses) from your ITE university. This is the person who may visit you in school.

Each person's ITE is unique and each trainee is different because you all have different experiences and different expertise. All training routes try to take this into account. You may have some experience of teaching in, perhaps, English as a Foreign Language (EFL) or a private school but find the demands of planning unfamiliar curricula challenging. Or you may be very familiar with the curriculum having been, say, a classroom assistant but find the management demands and performance aspect of teaching on placement a challenge. Each trainee will find some standards easier to address than others. This is why you will have some sort of *Individual Training Plan* to guide you through your course. This may be called a 'Professional Development Record', a 'training record' or something else. But it will be the document you use to set and monitor your targets. It will contain references to useful aspects of your prior experience as well as what you achieve during your training. Learning to use this sort of plan is important to succeeding in your ITE. It is also an important professional skill because you will have to do this sort of target setting and evidence collection throughout your probationary year and the rest of your career.

Short placements

One special type of professional placement you may encounter will be the short visit to another educational setting. You may visit a secondary school to look at the secondary curriculum in action, or to focus on transition to secondary school. You might visit a Nursery to look at the transition issues involved. You might visit a school with a particularly good teacher of one subject, or good practice in teaching children with English as an Additional Language (EAL) or Special Educational Needs (SEN). If you visit these sessions for a very short period you will not be expected to teach in them but you will usually be given tasks to focus your attention on particular aspects of practice.

The responsibilities of professional placement

All those involved in professional placement (mentors, trainees, link tutors) take on responsibilities that are discussed in detail later in this book. One type of responsibility raises particular ethical issues – that is, your responsibility to the children in your class. When you are working in a class you are participating in the education of all the children in that class and they will not get that time, or even that lesson, again. You have a responsibility as a teacher from the moment you begin your ITE. This includes the responsibility to ensure the children are learning as they should. Your class have the right to expect that you know how to behave in school, are well prepared and are able to seek the help and support you need. This book will help you to be well prepared and knowledgeable.

Full registration – your driving licence

The achievement of the Standards for Full Registration (SFR) may seem like a distant and demanding goal but remember that it is also only a beginning. Full registration is rather like a teacher's driving licence. When you achieve the standard for full registration you have achieved your driving licence and are safe to be let loose on a class relatively unsupervised. Like a novice driver, you are not an expert and will continue learning.

Achieving the Standard for Initial Teacher Education is a big step in your career but only the first step on a long road. It will be followed by a period of probation, further school based training which will be assessed by staff in the school.

In your ITE, try not to set yourself unreasonable demands. During professional placement you will find that you have to juggle demands, do extra research, fill gaps and generally cope with change. This is a normal part of school life and your training. Do not try to demand perfection of yourself and remember that you learn from the less successful experiences as well as the brilliant successes. Do not let off days (and you will have them) get you down.

PRACTICAL TASK PRACTICAL TASK PRACTICAL TASK PRACTICAL TASK PRACTICAL TASK

Before you go further in this book, you should review a number of important documents.

- Your course handbook of guidance for your training. Check you know when the professional placements take place in your course and what is expected of you on each placement. Note anything that is unclear to discuss with your tutor or mentor at your next meeting.

- Look at your ITE plan. (This may be called a training record, record of professional development, monitoring file, etc.) As soon as you have started your ITE, this plan should contain background information about yourself, your targets and reports. Try to focus on the personal strengths you will be taking into your first placement.

- Look at the standards for the award of ITE (www.gtcs.org.uk) and ensure you are familiar with them. Identify any that you are unclear about and look them up in the guidance (available from the same site) that gives further information about each standard.

A SUMMARY OF **KEY POINTS**

> This book aims to help you to succeed at professional teaching placement in Early Years and Primary.

> If you are undertaking ITE you will be doing professional placements.

> Your placement will involve an ITE provider, mentor, class teacher, and possibly a course tutor.

> Your placements will be guided by your own training plan (or record of development).

> As soon as you start your training you assume professional responsibilities and the first of these is to understand your training plan and the professional standards for Initial Teacher Education.

Resources

The General Teaching Council for Scotland (GTCS) http://www.gtcs.org.uk/Home/home.asp The General Teaching Council for Scotland is the professional regulatory body for teachers in Scotland. They:

- maintain and enhance professional standards of Scotland's teachers;
- support new teachers through the Standard for Full Registration;
- work with partner organisations across the world.

Go to 'becoming a teacher' to find links to the university websites.

Teach in Scotland, http://www.teachinginscotland.com/tis/171.html, provides an information point and links for those considering this as a career. It provides information and links for non-graduates wishing to embark on teacher training, graduates looking for a career change and teachers from elsewhere who wish to transfer to Scotland.

1
Preparing for professional placement

This chapter aims to make you aware of how your placements are organised, what is expected of you and what you can expect of those involved in your placement. The chapter is focused on helping you prepare for a setting that is new to you.

By the end of this chapter you should:

- **understand the disclosure requirements before you can go into school;**
- **know how and why teaching placements are selected.**

Before you can work with children

Before sending any student out on a school placement or into any other situation where they will be in contact with children, the student must successfully undergo a full disclosure check. These checks are carried out by the Scottish Criminal Record Office Disclosure Service. To undertake the check, you will need to complete a form on which you must disclose any previous criminal convictions, cautions or bind-overs, irrespective of when they occurred. The second part of the form requires your signature to agree to a criminal record check. The purpose of this is to safeguard the children with whom you will be working. You do not have to declare any motoring offences for which you received a fine and up to three penalty points but all other offences must be declared. All criminal convictions are considered and none are considered spent – the Rehabilitation of Offenders Act 1974 does not apply in this instance.

The ITE provider will tell you what you need to do and will obtain your agreement before any checks are made. The check is usually completed before students begin their courses but there can be delays and when the student is to be sent on a placement or school day visit soon after beginning the course, there can be problems. If the disclosure is not successfully completed before you are due to go out into school, you will not be able to go.

Make sure you complete any forms you are given promptly.

Selecting professional placements

All universities running ITE will ensure you have placements in more than one school. This ensures you are prepared to teach in schools generally, rather than in just one particular school. It also offers you a much wider range of staff, children and resources to learn from. Here are some of the most frequently asked questions on this subject.

Frequently asked questions

1. 'How will my placements be selected?'

If you are pursuing a PGDE or BEd programme, your ITE provider will assign places that it has been allocated by the local authority placement scheme, in the training partnership school on the basis of the information it has been given by you and by the school. So, if you are asked to fill in a form with personal details and questions about travel and domestic arrangements, make sure you are specific. ITE providers will accommodate you as conveniently as possible, taking into account the following factors:

- your training needs (the age phase or school type you need, any specific targets you have to address during this placement);
- 7the range of professional placement offers from schools in the partnership;
- the number of trainees who need placement;
- the geography and your travel arrangements;
- the training history of the school (you will not be placed in a school with a poor record of training or a school that has just gone into special measures);
- your commitments (if you are part-time, not all placements will be suitable).

Professional placement carries the same professional demands as other jobs. You may have to make domestic arrangements to ensure you can meet those commitments. It is not reasonable to expect placements to be arranged around pet care.

2. 'There is a really convenient school at the end of my road. Why can't I just go there?'

Your placement school has been chosen first of all, to meet your training needs, not just for geographical reasons. Most places are allocated on the principle that since not everyone has a convenient school with training places at the end of their road, it is fairer if everyone has to travel some distance. An effort is usually made to provide places within reasonable reach of your accommodation. There may be other reasons why it is not appropriate for you to train at that school.

3. 'Why doesn't the school at the end of my road have training places?'

The University is allocated the training places it requires by the local authority. The University cannot select the schools in which it will be given places. Schools sort out problems they may have with taking students with the local authority not with the University

4. 'Can I choose my own school?'

No, you will be allocated a place by your University based on the places they have available. There are several reasons for this. The organisation of placement by request would be impossible with large numbers of students from several Universities all requiring placements at the same time. You are training to teach in all types of schools in your age phase, not just those you like. Your school must be chosen with a range of factors in mind and your training needs are the most important.

Do not approach schools yourself unless you are asked to do so – you may cause real professional offence.

5. 'I am doing a PGDE and have been assigned a placement at some distance. My friend is doing a placement much nearer my home. Can we swap?'

Check with the person who arranges placements. It may be possible to swap. But it may not, for good reasons. Either you or your friend may have training needs that dictate a need to place you in those schools. It may be that those schools can offer different age phases, or examples of particularly good practice. It may be that the travel arrangements of several trainees can be accommodated using this placement pattern. If the schools already know who to expect, changing places will cause inconvenience.

6. 'I will be doing a final placement in a school that has much more challenging behaviour than ours. Can I refuse this offer?'

You are training to be a teacher who can teach in all Primary (or Early Years) schools. If this school is satisfactory in HMIE terms and is part of the training partnership then it is probably a good training setting and you must take advantage of the training it offers. Remember, too, that a school in a challenging area may actually be very successful indeed and may offer you some excellent models of good practice. In this case you will have the chance to see successful behaviour policies in action and work with teachers who are used to this challenging setting – learn from the support they can give you.

PRACTICAL TASK PRACTICAL TASK **PRACTICAL TASK** PRACTICAL TASK **PRACTICAL TASK**

When you know which school you will be going to for your professional placement there are some things you should do before you visit the school.

Use the Internet to find out as much about the school as you can

- Search the HMIE site for the school's most recent HMIE report.
- How old is the HMIE report? Does this mean some things will have changed, or that another HMIE inspection is due?
- What weaknesses did HMIE identify? These may well be areas the school will be working on and may particularly benefit you.
- Find out whether the school has a website and see what it tells you about the school. You might also check www.ukschoolguide.com – this website is a directory of all schools based in the UK.
- How large is the school? Does it have a nursery? If you are aiming to look at transition between key stages this may offer you particular opportunities.
- What are the school's strengths? Some of these may be of particular interest to you.
- Does the school undertake particular events like residential trips that might affect you?

Check the location and travel arrangements for the school

If you are travelling to school by public transport, make the journey at the appropriate time of day before your placement. You can then make sure you allow enough time on the day itself. If you will be driving to school the same applies – check how long the journey actually takes; maps can be deceptive. When you know what your journey will be like you can make any domestic arrangements you need.

Explore the area around the school

When you get to the school take the time to explore the streets around it, ensuring that you choose a safe time to do so. Take a good look round so you can form some impressions about the lives of the children you will be teaching. You will also be able to identify what resources children will have experienced (such as shops, cafés, etc.) and what local features might be a part of your teaching (park, mosque, church, village hall, etc.).

Join a union

Join at least one of the main teaching unions. All offer free membership to trainees and this includes valuable insurance and advice about all sorts of professional matters. Joining a union is discussed fully on pages 16–17.

What to expect on your professional placement

When a school has accepted you for a professional placement, it has a commitment to ITE and is looking forward to training you during your placement. The training partnership will have a contract with the school that sets out what they can expect of you and what you can expect of the school. Look at your training programme or guidance and you will find this is set out for you. Each training partnership is different, so check your details carefully.

What to expect of your school mentor

The standards emphasise that you should act upon advice and feedback and be open to coaching and mentoring for a good reason. This will be your chief vehicle of learning through professional placement. The school may provide a mentor who will be a teacher who has undertaken training and takes a lead role in dealing with trainees in the school. Your mentor is crucial to your training on professional placement. In some schools your mentor may also be your class teacher, but often the mentor is a senior member of staff who can provide the sort of objective support that we all need from time to time. The role of the school mentor will vary depending on the level of partnership the school is engaged in, but in general you can expect the following.

Your mentor will:

- be your main point of contact with the school;
- know the school well, including the strengths of different members of staff, resources and opportunities;
- meet you on a regular basis to help you to set targets, evaluate progress, and identify experiences you want to have;
- know the professional standards for the ITE and how to help you demonstrate them;
- be aware of your workload and help you to plan it effectively so that you can meet your training needs;
- observe some of your teaching and give feedback;
- assess and report on your progress;
- be trained, know what to expect of trainees and pass information about trainees to other members of staff.

Many schools do not have a trained mentor with responsibility for students and the class teacher will be your mentor, often with support from a member of the senior management team.

These roles are discussed more fully in Chapter 6.

Contacts

Your mentor will know the dates and expectations of the placement before you arrive, and will also have a handbook of guidance for the placement as well as other training materials. However, it is a good idea to discuss the placement requirements clearly at the beginning.

Mentors can help you to complete school-based tasks you may have been set as part of the placement or work you have to do for a project. Although they may know about these in advance you must discuss them with your mentor and plan when to complete them.

In school your mentor is the person who can provide details of the school policies, staff, etc. (see Chapter 6). Your mentor can also arrange training experiences you might need: perhaps observing a particular teacher who is good at something you are trying to get to grips with, or arranging a demonstration or discussion with an IT co-ordinator. If there is something you particularly need to be involved in, such as National Tests or report writing, you should always discuss it with the mentor, who will help you to make arrangements.

On your first day you will probably meet your mentor before you are taken to your class.

Planning, teaching assessment and recording

Your mentor may agree a timetable with you. This is not quite as specific as it sounds because of your developing needs and the pace of school life. At first your timetable will involve a great deal of observation. As you learn more about the class the amount of teaching will increase.

Your class teacher or mentor will routinely plan for your involvement in the teaching of language, maths, science and ICT.

Observation of your teaching

Mentors may manage and participate in observation of your teaching but they may not do it all themselves. Class teachers and subject co-ordinators may observe your teaching sessions and give you written and/or verbal feedback. Discuss who will observe you and when.

Regular review meetings

Your mentor may meet regularly with you to discuss:

- observations and feedback;
- your performance against your targets;
- setting more specific targets;
- your school-based tasks (if you have any);
- your performance against the standards for ITE.

Assessment

As your placement progresses your mentor will usually take the lead in writing a report about your progress. Different courses give these reports different names (profiles, reports, assessments, etc.). This report will be linked to the standards for ITE and will make judge-ments about the strengths and weaknesses of your teaching and subject knowledge based on the evidence provided by observation feedback sheets, mentor meetings, discussion, observations by other staff and the contents of your files. If you are engaged on a very long placement there will usually be an interim report about halfway through the placement. The report will be read by you, the mentor and any course staff involved in your training and will be the basis of target setting for subsequent placement, further course-based work or for your probationary year.

What to expect of the class teacher

Throughout your placement the class teacher will provide most of your day-to-day support. At the beginning of any placement, you will be observing your class teacher very closely to see how he or she works with the children, what the rules and expectations of classroom behaviour are and how your teacher rewards and enforces these expectations. Your first job is to be aware of these things and to get to know the names of the children in the class. You also need to know about your class teacher's routines and commitments in the school.

When you work with your class teacher he or she will be responsible for:

- showing you class rules and procedures (often by example);
- modelling good practice in teaching;
- helping you to analyse and reflect on your practice;
- focusing your attention on pupils' learning;
- discussing your planning so that it meets the school's needs as well as yours, and helping you to pitch it right.

Your class teacher may also:

- observe lessons;
- give you written and oral feedback on your lessons;
- help you to develop self-evaluation strategies;
- monitor your files.

Your class teacher is your colleague, your model and your adviser. He or she will have a unique teaching style and by observing it you can learn valuable lessons. As you progress in your practice, the teacher will share lesson planning and share the teaching as well as supporting you in planning and teaching lessons.

What to expect of course tutors

The role of the course tutor in teacher training varies enormously from course to course and they have different titles – advisers, link tutors, visiting tutors, etc. You will need to be sure you know the structure of your course. Roles of the course tutors in placement may include:

- target-setting and approval;
- reviewing progress and targets;
- visiting the placement to observe your teaching and giving feedback;
- offering support for subject knowledge improvement;
- offering advice about teaching techniques;
- moderating mentor assessment and grading of your performance;
- offering support for the mentor in your training and assessment.

Target-setting or approval

In all courses you will be expected to set targets for your placement and agree these with either a course tutor or your school mentor. This is part of your personal professional development. These targets are discussed in more detail later, but you will be expected to link them to the standards for ITE. As you progress through your placement you will modify and add to your targets as you achieve some of them. See target-setting (Chapter 6).

Reviewing progress and targets

When you have completed a placement you need to review your progress against the targets you set and the standards for ITE. Use your placement report, any written feedback you have had, your file of plans and evaluations. Your course tutor may meet you to help you review the placement: if so, make sure you go to the meeting prepared. Make a frank assessment of whether or not you have met your targets and how well you have done. Identify the standards you still have to address. Consider your strengths and your weaknesses. As well as identifying targets, your tutors can help you identify what you should do to meet them. By engaging in this type of review you are addressing the standards for Professional reflection and communication (2.4.3).

Visiting the placement, observing your teaching and giving feedback

Course tutors will usually arrange to visit you on placement at least once. There will probably be a number of reasons for the visit. They will want to monitor:

- that you are well placed and that the placement is meeting your needs;
- that you are making progress on your placement by building up your planning, teaching and assessment experience;
- that you are reviewing and achieving your targets;
- that you and your mentor are making the arrangements necessary to meet your targets;
- that you are doing any tasks you have been asked to do;
- that you are developing confidence;
- that your mentor is happy with your progress.

Support for subject knowledge improvement and teaching techniques

A visiting tutor may be able to suggest experiences you need to develop your teaching or subject knowledge. For instance, you might need to begin to teach the mental/oral section of a maths lesson, to observe a subject specialist in another class or work with a support for learning teacher. These arrangements can be made with your mentor.

Moderating mentor assessment and grading of your performance

On most courses, a tutor will visit to observe a lesson you are teaching. The tutor may do a joint observation with the mentor or teacher. This serves two purposes. First, the course tutor will offer you written feedback to assist your target-setting. Second, a joint observation will also have moderation value in the placement, ensuring that the tutor and mentor share opinions about your practice and expectations about what you should be achieving.

Support for the mentor

Course tutors will see many teachers and trainees teaching. They can help mentors to pinpoint the most effective experiences for you.

What the school is expecting of you

The school is committed to ITE so they are looking forward to your placement. The school mentor is expecting you to come to the placement with a professional attitude: most mentors would cite this as your most important quality. What is a professional attitude? It is the hallmark of a professional (of any type) that they aim to review and improve their work, develop their skills and abilities and take responsibility for their work and professional development.

- You need to be enthusiastic and committed to your chosen training. Enthusiasm and commitment produce positive responses from staff and pupils alike.
- You need to show your enthusiasm and commitment by being well prepared and working hard. This will earn the respect and support of your colleagues and make your lessons go well. Nothing upsets colleagues more than a trainee who is constantly trying to avoid work or leave early.
- You need to be willing to ask for help and information in a polite and friendly manner, and to choose an appropriate person and moment to do so.
- You need to be sensitive to the stresses that all teachers occasionally feel – five minutes before a tricky lesson is not the time to ask the teacher of that lesson for help.
- You need to be reasonably self-critical and able to accept criticism and advice as a learning experience. No one learns without some less-than-perfect lessons. No one will expect you to have all the answers.
- You need to feel you are directing your training and balancing your needs with the needs of the teachers and children. No one will respect you if, at the end of a placement, you have not done specific tasks because you 'didn't get round to it'.

Evidence of a professional attitude comes from a number of signs that you give in the early contacts with the school.

Appropriate dress is important. Different schools have different codes of dress for staff and these are usually unspoken rules. On your first visit it is worth being smart, but practical. Look at how the other teachers dress (perhaps on the school website). You will be setting an example to the children on behalf of the school and representing the school's values. Do not dress in a way that might upset children, parents or colleagues. Avoid immodest clothes and unusual hairstyles and remove obvious piercings. You will need to consider certain aspects of appearance for health and safety reasons. Long hair needs to be held back so that you have a clear all-round view, otherwise you cannot do the job. Your nails need to be short enough to help children in, say, gymnastics without spiking them. Dress like a member of the profession you want to join but do not feel you have to be super smart or purchase a whole new wardrobe.

Punctuality is also extremely important. Although the children will probably arrive between 8.30 and 8.55 a.m., the staff will be arriving at school much earlier. If you arrange to arrive early at school in order to meet your mentor, he or she will have set aside some time for you. That time is precious so make sure you are there and ready to make the most of it.

Confidentiality is another important professional characteristic. As a trainee teacher you must show the same degree of confidentiality that is expected of other teachers. This means that what happens in school is confidential within the school. You can usually talk and write about school events within the training partnership. You would certainly want to do so in course essays, for example, but even then names of children, staff and schools should be disguised.

You need to express yourself professionally and not make unsupported, sweeping or uninformed judgements.

In discussions within school you should avoid criticising your fellow teachers and gossiping about colleagues. This is just as important outside the staff group. Staff rooms contain a good many adults who are not members of school staff – visiting parents, advisers, inspectors, etc., and you need to remember this. You should not discuss school inappropriately with friends or relations

MINI CASE MINI CASE MINI CASE **MINI CASE** MINI CASE MINI CASE **MINI CASE**

The importance of confidentiality was brought home to Christine, a fourth-year BEd student, in an uncomfortable way. Christine had undertaken a placement in the school the previous term and had discussed it with a friend whose child attended the placement school. At some point Christine unwittingly expressed a negative opinion of the teaching skills of Mr X. The following term Christine's friend approached the school and asked that her son should not be put into Mr X's class, because of what she had heard. Naturally, the head teacher of the school was very upset. She felt that Christine had acted unprofessionally and damaged the reputation of the school. Christine was aghast and realised that she had, unintentionally, acted extremely unprofessionally. This was certainly not the sort of evidence of team working and collaboration she wanted to accumulate towards meeting the standards. She could only write apologising to the school and learn a hard lesson.

All this seems a tall order at first, but as long as you go to school positive and well prepared, you will find your school welcoming. Your school has the right to expect you to come to a placement with:

- a developing knowledge of the standards for ITE against which you will be assessed;
- an informed knowledge about your course of training – you should have read your course and placement handbooks;
- a clear idea of what your targets are for this placement; (On first placements this is much harder than in subsequent placements because everything is a target. Do not be afraid to discuss it with your mentor and set narrower targets such as specific observations or taking parts of lessons.)
- a clear picture of what you want to get out if the placement, not just from the point of view of the course and the standards, but on a personal level;
- an expectation of participating in assessment and planning meetings;
- an expectation of participating in staff meetings and training days, although you may not have much to contribute at first;
- your training plan or record of professional development;
- a school placement file.

REFLECTIVE TASK

Prepare your documentation for school placement. You will usually have a school placement file and a file about your professional development such as a professional development plan or monitoring file. You might be asked to combine these.

Prepare your school placement file

This is a file that you will use day-to-day to hold notes on school policies, plans, evaluations, assessments, etc. At first your school placement file will not contain a great deal but it will indicate that you have given the placement some thought and begun your preparation. When setting up a placement file you need to read the course documentation very carefully and think about your targets. This will help you to decide the sections you will need in a file and how to arrange them. Before you get to school for a first placement a placement file may simply have the following:

- your details;
- details of the school (including HMIE reports);
- file dividers for various sections (school policies, medium-term plans, weekly plans, daily plans, lesson evaluations, assessments, notes of mentor meetings, etc.);
- course details, including relevant sections of the course handbook;
- any forms needed for the placement, possibly as part of your record of professional development or training plan.

This is not in-depth material but it is a strong indicator of your attitude. A trainee who arranges this before the placement sends out strong messages of positive professional values like organisation. It shows you are committed and willing to work hard.

Prepare your training plan file (or professional development profile)

This document will have your background details in it, the standards for ITE and will develop to form a full record of your training. This file will probably be where you record the targets you set for the placement with the mentor or link tutor. At the start of a placement you should expect to spend some time reviewing this record. Use the format you are given as part of your training to:

- identify what you have already achieved in relation to the standards;
- identify key standards which you aim to meet (2.4.3).

You will discuss your record with your mentor at the school of the placement.

You will do a good deal more with this file after the placement, when you may want to put lesson plans, lesson observations, assessments and photographs into it.

Union membership

Most teachers belong to one of the main teaching unions (contact details on pages 18 and 146). These are trade unions that negotiate on behalf of their members on issues such as pay and conditions. However the unions also offer a wider range of additional services. Most of the unions produce materials especially for trainee teachers and probationary teachers. These range from advice about classroom management to tips for getting a job. The publications are often free to trainees and many trainees have found them invaluable. The unions also offer services such as insurance cover as part of membership. Each package is different but may provide insurance cover for:

- personal accidents;
- hospitalisation;
- personal property (including spectacles);
- malicious damage to motor vehicles in school or college premises.

The membership may also include the union's legal services in the case of any dispute and the services of the union in agreeing your pay package when you take up a job.

There are also additional benefits such as:

- discount shopping;
- life assurance and investments;
- mortgage facilities;
- legal services;
- credit card facilities;
- personal loans;
- motor insurance;
- motor breakdown and recovery services;
- travel facilities;
- tax recovery services;
- magazines;
- pocket diaries, calendars and pens, etc.

We strongly recommend you join at least one union before going into school for the insurance benefits as well as the excellent advice. Membership is usually free for trainees and some probationary teachers. Each union has slightly different policies and, eventually, you will want to be a member of a union that represents your view but, as a trainee, you do not have to make a final decision about which union because you can join them all. If you are doing a PGDE or degree course, the university may well have arranged contact with the unions. If not, they can be contacted at the URLs listed below.

The unions will have local branches and you may find that in many schools all the staff belong to one union but you can decide about this when you are probationary teacher.

MINI CASE MINI CASE MINI CASE **MINI CASE** MINI CASE MINI CASE **MINI CASE**

I only joined the unions because they were all there in the university one day and they were giving out good leaflets and pens and I really didn't expect to need them. On my very first placement my car was badly scratched in the school car park. On placement you are quite tense anyway and I found it really upsetting. I had already had a recent insurance claim and risked losing my no claims bonus if I claimed on the car policy. I also didn't want to make a fuss in school or draw attention to myself. The union said I was covered through them and they paid out for the repairs with very little effort on my part. Since then I have had the magazines and booklets they send, which have been good, especially in helping me to prepare interviews. I also consulted them about my starting salary. I will retain membership of all three unions this (my probationary) year then decide which to go for when I have to pay.

Nahid, NQT

A SUMMARY OF **KEY POINTS**

> Your placements are chosen with your training needs and circumstances in mind and should include a range of experiences for you.

> You should do a little research about your school before you start.

> Your mentor is a member of the school staff who will know about your training and will work to support you through your placement.

> Your class teacher will be your principle model of good practice and will teach with you.

> Course tutors will participate in your training, moderating, offering advice and training.

> From the very beginning of your placement you must act professionally. This means having a professional attitude, being punctual, maintaining confidentiality and dressing appropriately.

> We strongly suggest you join at least one teaching union before beginning placement.

Resources

Association of Teachers and Lecturers www.atl.org.uk. ATL, formerly the Assistant Masters and Mistresses Association (AMMA), is a fully democratic, TUC-affiliated trade union and professional association.

Educational Institute of Scotland www.eis.org.uk/. The EIS is the largest organisation of teachers and lecturers in Scotland representing around 80 per cent of the profession in nursery, primary, special, secondary and further and higher education.

National Association of School Masters/Union of Women Teachers www.teachersunion.org.uk. NASUWT is one of the largest teaching unions and the only one to organise in England, Wales, Scotland and Northern Ireland. NASUWT has members in all sectors of education and represents teachers in all roles including heads and deputies.

National Union of Teachers www.teachers.org.uk/index.php. The NUT is the largest of all the teaching unions. It is a professional association and a trade union that also provides access to a variety of conferences and reference materials for teachers and staff within the education sector. Membership for students is free.

Professional Association of Teachers www.pat.org.uk/. This independent trade union caters for all workers in education. Founded in 1970 it has approximately 35,000 members.

Teachernet www.teachernet.gov.uk/professionaldevelopment/professionalassociations/unions. Teachernet is the DfES site for teachers. it contains information for teachers about all aspects of professional life. You can link to all the unions from this site.

The Scottish Criminal Record Office Disclosure Service has more details about disclosure on their website at www.disclosurescotland.co.uk

2
Starting in school

In this chapter we aim to help you gather information in a setting that is new to you. Even if you have considerable experience in schools you may benefit from taking a close look at the culture and organisation.

By the end of this chapter you should:

- **know the purpose of preparation days;**
- **know what to find out about your school;**
- **know what information to collect about your class;**
- **be able to observe in the first days in your class.**

Placement preparation days in school

Before you start the main body of a professional placement, or at the start of that placement, you will spend a few days in the school to get used to the setting. This may be one day a week for several weeks or it may be a few days in a single week. However your preparation time is organised, this time is crucial in enabling you to be ready to make the most of a professional placement.

In those first few days it is important to get to know the school and you should expect members of staff to help you to do that. The school mentor will arrange the first few days in a new situation so that you can:

- tour the school, perhaps with children;
- have a copy of the school prospectus;
- learn tips about the school routines (such as timetables, lunch arrangements, etc.);
- learn the rules for photocopying and use of resources;
- see and note the school behaviour and Health and Safety policies;
- learn the first aid procedures;
- learn the fire drill procedures (for your class);
- set up regular mentor meeting times;
- learn about your class.

Many schools will have a trainee teacher induction pack ready for you. This usually includes:

- the school handbook;
- guidance given to supply teachers about routines, break times, etc., school behaviour and health and safety policies;
- a staff list;
- a school map.

If your school does not have such a pack you should ask your mentor for access to these documents.

School layout and emergency exits

It is usual practice for the school mentor to show students around a school on an initial visit but in a large school this can leave you feeling overwhelmed by the sheer amount of information given. It is a good idea to obtain a copy of the school map and ask a small group of older children to take you on an additional tour during a lunch break. In this way you can proceed at your own pace and annotate the map with any notes that will be personally useful. It is also crucial that you know the location of fire exits of the area you will be working in and your assembly point outside the building. Identify these on the map and clarify the procedure for using them with your class teacher. You can build on this information by looking at the school health and safety policy.

Who's who?

When you join a school for a teaching placement you become a member of the school team, even if you are a temporary, junior member. Make a conscious effort to become acquainted with not only your class teacher but with other staff too. The school staffing list may be extensive, so make short notes next to names to help you remember who's who. Try to learn names, starting with those of your mentor, teacher, teaching assistant(s) and head teacher and notice how staff members address each other – it would be unfortunate to call your head teacher by his first name if the class teacher always calls him Mr – . A little polite conversation will usually allow you to find out what your mentor's and class teacher's areas of responsibility are within the school, what age group or sets they teach and which parts of their work they enjoy most.

It is essential to know the names and roles of any parallel class teachers and support staff. You will be working closely with them – observing their practice, planning, sharing resources – and may teach lessons with them. You will also want to learn the names of a wider circle of teachers over the first week or so of the placement. The Additional Support for Learning Co-ordinator will be an important member of staff who can tell you about processes for children with ASL, show you some Individual Education Plans (IEPs) and discuss arrangements made to meet the needs of a range of children. There will also be subject co-ordinators for some subjects in the Primary curriculum. Knowing and understanding the roles of colleagues with specific responsibilities is part of the standards (Element 1.2.2). You may want to learn from these members of staff later in the placement by, for instance, observing particularly good guided reading by the language co-ordinator or a dance lesson led by the PE co-ordinator. Arrangements of this type are usually made through your mentor and you should discuss them with the mentor in the first instance.

Look beyond the classroom and introduce yourself to staff in the office and the lunchtime supervisors who work directly with the children. This will allow you to appreciate the school community properly and established, knowledgeable staff are more likely to support and advise a student who makes an effort to be friendly than one who shuts themselves away in their classroom.

Important routines – assemblies, movement about the school and lunchtime

One of the most important, and obvious, pieces of information you need is the timing of the school day. This information may well be in your welcome pack but if it is not, make sure you note on your first day:

- school starting and finishing times;
- when staff arrive and leave the school;
- the times of break times and lunchtime;
- assembly times;
- the weekly staff meeting time;
- any regular phase or planning meetings.

These form the basic structure of the day but you will also want to observe the teachers' routines over your first week. Most teachers arrive some time before the children start and leave some time after school finishes. They will all stay on to attend staff meetings. You should expect to do the same and you may well find that, early in your career, you need extra time to accomplish your preparation. If your school has staff training days for the whole school staff it is important that you take part in these, although as a trainee you should expect to keep a low profile. Participating in these aspects of school life shows your professional commitment.

Try to observe and learn the school's social rituals. On your first day ask what the arrangements are for paying for coffee and tea and offer to contribute. Notice when the teachers congregate in the staff room and when they stay in their rooms to prepare. There will not be time for you to leave school premises during the day. Do not expect to be able to pop out to the shops at lunchtime or make personal arrangements during school time. If school staff bring a packed lunch or have school dinners, do the same. Most teachers spend a very short time in the staff room at lunchtime but they will usually choose the same times to do their preparation and all use the beginning, middle or end part of lunchtime to congregate in the staff room. It is important to participate gradually in these routines. In a Nursery there may be very little time at break time or lunchtime and staff may have a rota for these occasions. It is important to notice when the staff do meet to chat and mentors will see your willingness to participate as part of Element 1.2.2 – working as a team member.

There will be wider opportunities for child-orientated activities. Breakfast and after-school clubs are common and you should find out about them. You will also, gradually, want to find out about after school or lunchtime activities. Your knowledge of French, chess, rugby or line dancing might be useful and allow you to contribute later in the placement.

MINI CASE MINI CASE **MINI CASE MINI CASE** MINI CASE **MINI CASE**

We'd all made the usual jokes about not sitting in the deputy head's chair before the placement but, really, going into the staff room for the first couple of times on all my placements was a bit nerve-wracking. My first school was huge and the staff room seemed vast. I felt very conspicuous. Everyone pretty much ignored me and just made their own tea and put the cups in the dishwasher. My mentor sort of waved me on and said 'help yourself'. I didn't say a word for the first few times in there but gradually I found I could join in the general chit chat. The staff sort of included me and I can see, looking back, that their lack of fuss was actually reassuring. I didn't spend much time in the staff room – about 15–20 minutes at lunchtime, maximum – but after five weeks I was really at home. I see now how important it was to be part of the staff in that way.

Jennie, PGDE

MINI CASE MINI CASE MINI CASE **MINI CASE** MINI CASE MINI CASE **MINI CASE**

I had been a classroom assistant, so I was used to schools but I did find I talked about different things in the staff room during my placements. In a few minutes at lunchtime I could ask all sorts of things and sort out resources. I enjoyed the familiarity but it felt different.

John, PGDE

MINI CASE MINI CASE MINI CASE **MINI CASE** MINI CASE MINI CASE **MINI CASE**

My placement was in a nursery school so even with the nursery nurses and teachers on a rota there were only really three of us in the staff room at lunchtime or on breaks. I was surprised that this worked so well, but it did mean that planning meetings were even more important. I think that it is really vital to remember to take your breaks for tea and keep your energy levels up.

Pat, BEd.

Teachers may be involved in some routine duties such as corridor supervision or bus loading duties. These are important times for supervision of the children but most of all a very important time for you to see the children outside the very formal setting of the class. You should go with your class teacher when they do these duties. You might ask to go out with your mentor or a member of the management team.

PRACTICAL TASK PRACTICAL TASK PRACTICAL TASK PRACTICAL TASK PRACTICAL TASK

Ask if you can accompany a member of staff on playground duty. Choose a day when you have already met your class and know them a little.

As you go out ask:

- Who does playground duty?
- What is his/her main purpose in doing duty?
- What are the behaviour rules for children in the playground?
- What, if any, equipment is provided?
- Who is the first-aider and what is the procedure for cuts and grazes?

Notice how the supervisors (usually classroom assistants and management) circulate round the area and talks to groups of children.

- How does the supervisor appear friendly with them?
- How does the supervisor, at the same time, maintain a professional relationship?

You need actively to imitate these strategies so that the children will chat with you but not be too familiar. You should discourage gratuitous cuddling, children's hands in your pockets and over-personal questions. Children will try these as ways to test your role as a teacher.

Observe the children at play. For many of them, playtime is the most important part of the day and it is certainly the time when most social learning is going on – how to make and keep friends, turn taking, joining and leaving groups, negotiation and compromise. Playtime may also involve a little mild violence or psychological torture (mostly about friendship) and you have a role here in preventing bullying and helping children to sort things out.

Observe what the children do at playtime.

- Do different groups do different things?
- Does there seem to be a difference in activity related to age or gender?
- Look at children you know and see who plays together.
- Are there any children on their own? Do they seem happy?
- Who complains of being left out? How can you help them to take part?
- Are the children using the equipment – climbing toys, sand pits, markings, skipping ropes, etc?
- Which children use them?
- What games are being played (ball rhymes, skipping rhymes, variations on tag, etc.)?

Observing your class in the playground can give you a much greater understanding of some children.

Moving around the school and class

Notice how the children move around the school. This is a very rule-governed business and recognising the rules (and when someone is breaking them) is one of the things that identifies you as a teacher to the children. On your first day notice how the children use the corridors (no running, letting others pass nicely) and be prepared to ask children to do this.

There are also basic rules for moving around in your class.

- In an Early Years setting, what are the processes for settling children on the mat?
- In a Nursery setting, what are the rules for behaviour on the mat?
- During seatwork, when are the children allowed to leave their seats?
- When they are sent to get an item in class, how are they supposed to move, and what are the sanctions for running, etc?
- When you want to accomplish a transition, such as moving from the mat to groups, what is the procedure and best way to give instructions?
- What key words should you include in instructions to move around?
- When the teacher sends children to get something, note how he or she avoids all the children rushing to the same place.
- What procedure is used when moving into another class or area? Do the children line up?
- When moving into the hall for PE, do the children do something specific, like finding a space?
- When the teacher sends a child to another place with a message, register or other task, what is the routine? Is it a privileged job? Does more than one child always go?

These are small but important details and observing them will establish your role as a teacher.

In my first placement I didn't really establish myself with the class and I felt they saw me as a helper – not a teacher at all. It shrivelled my confidence. On my next placement I asked my next mentor for advice before I even went into class. She told me to start by moving groups around as part of the lessons my teacher was teaching that day. I worked with my teacher to do this on my second day. It set me up. I began by showing a bit of authority, with my teacher there to support me, and I built on it. On my third day I lined the class up and took them into the hall for assembly. It took a bit of time to get silence and some naming of individuals to keep it but I felt it was the one act that established my role and set me up for really teaching that class.

Abby, Second Year BEd.

Taking photographs in school

A small but important aspect of your ICT work will be taking photographs in school. As part of your assessment evidence, especially at pre-5 and infant stages you (and the children) may well take photographs of children and you will certainly take photographs of assemblies and school visits. These photographs can be shared with the children for discussion, discussed with parents and may go into displays, children's work and school newsletters and websites. The use of photographs is governed by the school policy and professional responsibility. The school will have a policy about the use of photographs that aims to protect the identity of children and of the school. You must read it and adhere to it.

You should also ask your teacher to take photographs of you teaching in a way that adheres to the school photography policy. Photographs of you teaching a class masterfully, using the interactive whiteboard, working sensitively in the dramatic play area, reading with a group, accompanying a school visit or assisting at cookery are not only excellent in supporting your evidence towards the standards for ITE, but also go down very well at interviews for teaching posts.

When you use photographs of yourself teaching for displays, ensure that all children are not identifiable and that the school name cannot be identified from the photographs. If it is on the school sweatshirt you may have an interesting ICT challenge smudging this part of the image.

Your class group(s)

On your placement you will have a key teacher and class but this might mean different things in different placements.

Early Years settings have a number of different ways of organising their work. All of them will involve teachers and nursery practitioners planning together and teaching together.

- Nursery classes can be an ordinary class in the school with a nursery teacher and nursery nurse.
- Nursery classes may be part-time or have two shifts of children, those who come in the morning and those who come in the afternoon, with a few who stay all day.

Whatever the organisation, you will be assigned to one teacher and will be gradually taking over his or her role in the planning, teaching, management and assessment of this class.

For Early Years this means working very closely with the team of nursery practitioners or classroom assistants and you will have to be very careful to identify the teacher's special role in the team. This is not as easy as it sounds.

In infant placements you may find a number of ways of organising classes. P1 classes will not exceed 25 children (under review), most of them will have a single teacher and some may have a part-time or full-time classroom assistant or nursery nurse. In P2 and above, classes will not exceed 33 children and if the classes are composite – combine children from two or more stages – they may not contain more than 25 children.

- The most common organisation for P1 or P2 is one teacher per class.
- Some classes may be composite comprising children at P1 and 2 or P2 and 3.
- In small schools, particularly those in rural areas, classes may be composite for three or more stages although the number of children in the class will be low.
- In some schools with larger intakes, there may be setting where children are re-grouped across classes for maths and language and in some cases other subjects. You will usually work with the set your teacher would take and have the extra challenge of getting to know children from other classes.
- If the school is of an open-plan design, you may find the children have a 'home' teacher to whom they report first thing in the morning but may then move into a variety of groupings with a number of teachers or other members of staff throughout the day.

From P2 upwards, you may have classes of up to 33 children unless it is a composite class in which case you will have a maximum of 25 children. Each class has a teacher and some time from a classroom assistant. You may have:

- a single year class that does all subjects with the teacher;
- a single year class that does most subjects with the teacher but has some specialist teaching in music, PE or some other subject;
- a mixed year class that may do all subjects, or some with the same teacher;
- mixed year or single year classes that set for language, mathematics and sometimes science. This is very common in upper primary, especially in schools with more than one class per stage. In practice it means that the children all go to pre-arranged classes for mathematics and language at an agreed time. The sets may be organised by ability and children may be in different sets for language and mathematics. You will usually work with the set for which your class teacher has responsibility but your training needs might require that you work with a different set. For example, if you wanted to develop your differentiation for able pupils, you might work with a top set.

Meeting the class

Whatever class you are placed in, your first step will be meeting the class teacher and simply watching the class for a day, perhaps helping children to complete tasks. Your introduction to the class is very important. The children will use your title and surname (unless first names are used for all teachers in the school) and the teacher will tell the children you will be teaching them for some of this term. You must look confident and relaxed, however terrified you feel, and fill the role of teacher as you are introduced. Stand up straight and keep your arms relaxed (it may help to hold a file or something to stop you nervously clasping your hands). Smile – a relaxed, authoritative smile is appropriate, not a nervous whimper or a rictus grin. Any time you say something it must be confident and authoritative: 'I am looking forward to teaching you' rather than a weak 'Hello'. First impressions count and you need to signal to the class that you know what you are doing – even if you are not really that sure of yourself.

During your initial visits, obtain class lists for all the groups of children you will be working with. Then take time to annotate these lists from your observations and in discussion with the class teacher. His or her observations will be very useful and enable you to begin to formulate a class picture before actually working with the children. The checklist below suggests possible queries for you to observe or discuss with your class teacher.

- How many children are there in the class?
- Who is full-time/part-time/morning or afternoon (for nursery)?
- What sets are there and who is in which?
- How are the class seated? Do they choose a spot or are they assigned chairs? If they generally stay in the same places, making a seating map will help you learn names.
- Which children are on the school's ASL register? How does their special need manifest itself? How does the class teacher plan for inclusion?
- Which children in the class have been identified as more able? In which subject(s) is the child gifted? What strategies does the class teacher utilise to ensure they are reaching their full potential?
- Which children have EAL? What other language do they speak? What arrangements are made to support them?
- Which children find difficulty in controlling their behaviour? Is this related to an identified support need? What steps does the class teacher take to manage the child's behaviour? Is there a reward system? What will happen if the child needs to be removed from the classroom as a result of its behaviour?
- Are there any sensitive issues about any child's family circumstances you need to be aware of (e.g. recent bereavement, divorce, parental custody or child protection concerns)? Remember you are expected to treat this information with the highest degree of confidentiality.
- Are there any children with medical problems that you should be aware of? For example are there any children with asthma, epilepsy or allergies? Where are the inhalers kept? Who is qualified to administer a child's epi-pen? Who are the school's first-aiders? What procedure should you follow if a medical incident occurs during your lesson?
- Which friendship groupings are conducive to learning and which are not?
- What teaching assistance does the teacher have? When do classroom assistants work with the class? When do classroom assistants work with particular children? What are the roles of classroom assistants in this class? Are there any other adults working in the class?

As you spend your first day in the class you will begin to learn children's names and to see how they work.

PRACTICAL TASK PRACTICAL TASK PRACTICAL TASK PRACTICAL TASK PRACTICAL TASK

Observe a daily routine. On the first day in school you need to note as many class routines as you can. Use one of these question lists to guide your first observations, then supplement these in discussion with your teacher. Make a note of times at each transition point.

Early Years setting

- How (and when) do the children come into the building?
- How do staff greet parents and how long do parents stay?
- Is the first activity of the day set up? When? By whom?

- How do children know where to go?
- Which adults manage which tasks? Who is outside?
- Are outdoor clothes such as wellington boots and coats used? What is the routine?
- How do adults participate in play tasks?
- How is a change of task signalled? (Music, clapping, hands in air, etc.)
- How many children are allowed to do each activity at a time? How do they know?
- What is the routine for fruit time? Who prepares it? What do the children do? What language is used?
- What are the routines for using the lavatory and hand washing? (If any children in the setting wear nappies, ask your teacher for advice.)
- When do the children gather for group (or class) time on the mat?
- What do children do for packing up time? How is this signalled?
- When are stories and rhyme routines done?
- What arrangements are there for children taking books home (or story sacks) and changing them?

P1–7
- How (and when) do children come in from the playground and what are they expected to do as they come in?
- How does the teacher settle the class to attention?
- Who takes the register? How do children respond? What do the children do as it is taken? What happens to the register?
- Is there an assembly? Does the teacher attend?
- What are the lesson times?
- How does each lesson start and finish?
- Which other adults work in the class during teaching times and what do they do?
- How are resources (pencils, books, etc.) arranged? Who collects them?
- How does the teacher get the children's attention?
- How does the teacher move children from the mat to tables?

Timetable, curriculum, resources and behaviour

In your first few days you will have the chance to talk to your mentor and your teacher.

If you have a mentor she will play a lead role in the school's involvement in the partnership for training. This means the mentor will be familiar with the standards for ITE, even if the rest of the staff are not. Your mentor will also have contact with the university involved in your training. So your mentor will know the arrangements for your placement and the requirements (generally) of this placement – which key stage you need to be in, when you will be arriving and something of your previous experience. The mentor will also know their role in helping you to become established, observing, arranging meetings with you and reviewing progress. Usually, the mentor will have the report forms that may be required about your progress, but in some courses you will take these into school yourself.

Your mentor will be keen to know about you and will certainly want to set, or see, specific targets for this placement. On some courses, you may decide on these with a course tutor before the placement. In others you will set these with the mentor early in the placement. Either way, meeting these targets, showing your mentor evidence that you have met the targets, and setting new targets are important elements of your relationship. So your first mentor meeting will focus on:

- discussing the requirements for the placement and personal targets for your placement;
- helping you to get information about the school;
- answering your questions so far.

You will also meet your teacher. Key topics for discussion with him/her will be the timetable of the class, planning for class teaching and managing behaviour.

Having observed a day in class, you will have ideas about the rough timings of the day. To draw up a timetable you need to check these and add hall and PE times, times when any sets meet, times when the class is booked into an ICT suite and times when other teachers take the class. You can then put in the teacher's intended teaching times. These may be simply language, mathematics and cross-curricular themes, or each subject may have an identified time. Many schools block some subjects into different terms, so your class may do art one term and design and technology (D&T) the next. You will also need to know what teaching assistance you have in and out of the classroom and who will work with children during your lessons.

In Early Years settings you will have a broad idea of the pattern of activity from observation and you need to discuss with the teacher how the learning is addressed. Do different staff manage different areas? Does each member of staff plan activities for each area? You need to know which activities the children are encouraged to do and which are a matter of choice. How is this monitored?

The planning of the teaching is your next area of interest. Establish what topics are to be taught and what associated learning outcomes need to be achieved in each curriculum subject during your placement. Obtain copies of any relevant medium- and short-term plans and look at these with your class teacher. He or she will identify lessons for you to observe and be sure you know whether you are expected to take part in them. Planning is discussed in more detail in Chapter 3.

When you have identified the lessons, or parts of lessons, you will teach on the timetable, it is essential to be prepared. The following checklist will help.

- Find out where the school stores the curriculum resources (this will take a little time). Which resources are classroom based and which are kept centrally? Once located, you can select resources applicable to your identified teaching objectives and refer to them in your planning.
- What computers are available? Will you have an electronic whiteboard, computers in the class, laptops or access to a suite of computers? In the first few days at school arrange a time with the IT co-ordinator to examine how the school manages its toolbox of software.
- Assess whether new resources need to be made in order to achieve the learning objective. Any new resources you create should be relevant and child friendly.
- Is a worksheet necessary? If so, when you create it make sure it allows children to demonstrate their understanding rather than just filling in boxes.

- If you need to use photocopied resources for your lesson find out the school's procedure for photocopying. Will administration staff or teaching assistants organise photocopying for teaching staff or is it the teacher's responsibility? If it is the latter, make time to understand how the photocopier works.
- Who will help to prepare and locate resources and create displays? If you have a certain amount of administrative or teaching assistant time you need to know how much and whom you should go to. You also need to identify areas for your displays with the teacher.
- Be organised. Ensure your resources are ready before the lesson. Photocopy any material in plenty of time. Photocopiers have a habit of jamming, usually just before an observed lesson, so have your copied resources ready well in advance. Collect any centrally stored resources, such as lenses for a science lesson, well beforehand. This will avoid a potentially stressful situation when you realise ten minutes before a lesson that they have disappeared from the science cupboard.

To teach a class of children on initial teaching practices can be a daunting process, so if you take steps to be planned and prepared you can focus on developing your classroom management style without the additional worry of lesson content.

REFLECTIVE TASK

When you have done your initial days in your placement setting you should ask yourself how well you can address Element 1.2.2. 'Acquire a good working knowledge of the sector in which they teach and their professional responsibilities within it.'

Organise your notes under these headings:

- school policies;
- the school day (routines);
- rules of behaviour;
- learning needs of the classes;
- resources.

Review these notes at the end of your first week in school and ensure you have no gaps.

A SUMMARY OF **KEY POINTS**

> It is essential for you to spend a few days in school to gather information about the school and class.

> You may be placed with one year group but a number of other arrangements are possible, including sets, units and mixed age years.

> Find out about the school policies and read them early in your placement – all activity in school has to follow these policies.

> When you meet your class, create a professional, confident first impression.

> Learn school routines and staff habits. This will help you to feel at home.

> You should learn staff names and roles as soon as possible as you will be working with a number of people in school.

> In your first few days in school you should work out the class timetable and how you will fit in.

Resources

The government website LTS – http://www.ltscotland.org.uk/ has a wide range of supportive information for teachers. Use it to find out about the roles of staff in schools. You will also find all the relevant curriculum and assessment documents and advice on this site.

3
Learning to observe, plan and evaluate on teaching placement

By the end of this chapter you should know:

- **how to observe in a focused way;**
- **how medium-term, short-term and lesson plans are related;**
- **how to plan for parts of lessons and whole lessons;**
- **how to evaluate your lessons.**

When you have been in your placement school for a few days, whether it is your first or third placement, you will have collected a great deal of information and be ready to focus on the process of learning to teach successfully and meet the standards for ITE. Just as each school is different, each trainee is different. You will have a different background, different needs and so will require different experiences from your colleagues. The main techniques you will use to develop your teaching will be:

- **observation and discussion with teachers;**
- **planning;**
- **evaluating;**
- **teaching;**
- **assessing;**
- **completing school-based tasks.**

This chapter addresses observation, planning and evaluation.

Observation

Observation in your placement class(es) is particularly important because it is observation of what you are going to be doing very soon. The key thing to remember in all observations is that you are not observing to judge or criticise in a negative sense. You are observing to see:

- what children and teachers do in certain situations and with certain children;
- how certain actions and situations produce certain responses;
- how policies and theories work in practice;
- what you can learn from the situation.

The last point is the most important. You will not teach in the same way as anyone you watch but you will learn something from every lesson you observe. At the start of a placement there is something to be said for aping the teacher – or at least stepping into their shoes. The children in your class are used to certain routines and behaviours from their teacher, so you will appear authoritative and trustworthy to children if you know the routines and behave as they expect a teacher to behave.

The observation aspect of a placement is extremely important so do not rush through it. At the start of the placement you really need to observe everything – behaviour management, core subject teaching, assemblies, cross-curricular teaching, and staff meetings. Generally, you should observe a subject being taught before you teach it yourself. Some trainees overlook this in their enthusiasm to get going on the teaching part of the placement.

General observations

Early in a placement, you should do the following observations, making specific notes, then review your notes. These will enable you to make a start at teaching.

PRACTICAL TASK PRACTICAL TASK **PRACTICAL TASK** PRACTICAL TASK **PRACTICAL TASK**

Observing core subject lessons

Primary 1 to 7 – observe a language and a maths lesson

Use the form below as a prompt to observe the lesson. Make notes (or use a sheet of a similar layout) about as much as you can so that you get an idea of the structure the teacher and children are used to, the key vocabulary, how arrangements are made for different children's needs and what the routines of the lessons are.

Prompt sheet for observing literacy and maths	
Lesson outcome	P .... No. of children ....
At the beginning of the lesson	
Teaching strategies	Class management and control
How does the teacher introduce the lesson outcome? Does the teacher check prior knowledge, recall of previous material? How is the lesson set out to facilitate the start? Resources used? What do other adults in class do? Modelling of reading or writing? Mathematics games? Questioning? What is the balance of teacher-to-pupil talk? How long does this phase of the lesson last?	How does the teacher gain the children's attention and settle them? How does the teacher keep attention? What does the teacher do if a child is not paying attention? Evidence of pupils' interest and motivation?
During the lesson	
How do the pupils know what they will be doing? What sorts of tasks are they doing? Does the teacher work with one group or many? How do the other adults in the classroom work and with whom? Is there use of specific vocabulary? How are the pupils grouped? How are independent tasks related to the rest of the lesson? How long does this phase of the lesson last?	How does the teacher manage the transition from the mat (or group) to seat work? How do pupils get their resources? How does the teacher keep pupils on task? How does the teacher monitor the class? What 'rewards' does the teacher offer? (praise, eye contact, words, etc.) What sanctions does the teacher use? (frown, naming, etc.)
At the end of the lesson	
How does the teacher conclude the lesson? What learning does the teacher revisit? Which pupils report back on what they have done? How do pupils know how well they have done? How long does this phase of the lesson last? What do other adults in the class do? Is there homework? Is the next lesson referred to?	What is the signal for this phase of the lesson? How do pupils arrange their resources? How does the teacher manage the transition from seat work to the mat (or group)? Are pupils willing or enthusiastic to present their work? How does the teacher dismiss the class?

Early Years Setting – observe the teacher's role in a group session

Use one of the two forms below to observe a small group during one session. The first looks at one child activity, the second a whole session, involving more than one activity – possibly a practitioner-directed activity and a child-led activity. Observe as much as you can so that you get an idea of the routines the teacher and children are used to, the key vocabulary, how arrangements are made to include different children and what the learning objective of the session is.

Observing a practitioner working in an area of provision within the Early Years setting	
• Description of the area of provision (e.g. water/sand/role play area) • Information about the children involved (e.g. number, age, sex – is this a new activity for the children or one the children are very familiar with?) • Focus of the activity • What does the practitioner say and do? • What do the children say and do? • How does the practitioner monitor the children's achievements? How are children given feedback on their achievements? • Additional information, e.g. How long did the activity last? What did the children do next? What did the practitioner do next?	• Child interactions (non-verbal and verbal) • With self • With others • Actions including mark-making, drawing and any other recording included in the activity

Prompt sheet for observing an early childhood setting session	
At the beginning of the lesson	
Entry to the session	
Adult activity	Child activity
How does the teacher welcome and direct the children? Are there routine 'beginning' processes, such as going to the mat, returning books, etc? How is the lesson set out to facilitate the start? Resources used? What do other adults in class do? What does the teacher or other group leader do to direct children? What does the teacher or other group leader do to engage children? Questioning? What does the teacher do if a child is not engaged in an activity? What is the balance of teacher-to-pupil talk? What area of learning do the activities address?	How does the child know what is available? Does the child choose the activity or is the child directed? How does the teacher attract attention? Evidence of pupil's interest and motivation? Does the child interact with other children? What vocabulary does the child use? What resources does the child use? Is there a produce, such as drawing, writing, model? What happens to this?
Self-selected activity	
How does the teacher welcome and direct the children? Are there routine 'beginning' processes, such as going to the mat, returning books, etc? How is the lesson set out to facilitate the start? Resources used? What do other adults in class do? What does the teacher or other group leader do to direct children? What does the teacher or other group leader do to engage children? Questioning? What does the teacher do if a child is not engaged in an activity? What is the balance of teacher-to-pupil talk? What area of learning do the activities address? How does the child know what is available? Does the child choose the activity or is the child directed?	How does the teacher attract attention? Evidence of pupil's interest and motivation? Does the child interact with other children? What vocabulary does the child use? What resources does the child use? Is there a produce, such as drawing, writing, model? What happens to this?
Session conclusion	
How does the teacher conclude the lesson? What learning does the teacher revisit? Which pupils report back on what they have done? What vocabulary do pupils use? How long does this phase of the lesson last? How does the teacher manage the transition from seat work to the mat (or group)?	What is the signal for this phase of the lesson? How do pupils arrange their resources? Are pupils willing or enthusiastic to recall activities? How does the teacher move the group on?

The other key issue you will be involved with is managing the behaviour of the children in your class. This is dealt with later, in much more detail. At the moment, however, the chief priority is to make a good start with this particular group of children. Read the school's behaviour policy as soon as you can and be sure you understand it. Make notes of the key points and check your observations to see what elements of the policy you have already seen in action. Ask your teacher, very early on, what she expects from the class, what rules she applies and what rewards and sanctions she offers. Most teachers are so used to this they may have to think to recall what they actually do but you need to know, so watch and ask. You should set the same standards, enforce the same rules and offer the same rewards as your teacher. To do this you must know what they are!

By the end of your preparation days in schools you should know most of the following.

- What subjects and/or topics are being taught during your placement.
- The class routine.
- The names and broad characteristics of the children in your class, sets or groups.
- The school behaviour and Health and Safety policies and how these are implemented in your class.
- The names and roles of staff involved with your children.
- The daily routines of the class and school.
- Staffroom etiquette.
- The location and procedures for resources (in broad terms).

You should be able to participate in lessons and talk confidently to the children.

Primary 1 to 7

For these stages, you should make:

- at least one observation of the teacher's behaviour management in a mathematics and a language lesson (see Chapter 8);
- at least one observation of the teacher's behaviour management in an infant subject lesson (see Chapter 8);
- at least one observation of the teacher's behaviour management outside the classroom, the hall or the ICT suite (see Chapter 8);
- observations of mathematics, language and science lessons so that you can see the structures of these lessons (see Chapter 3);
- observations of break-time and lunchtime routines for the class.

Early Years Setting

For this stage, you should make:

- at least one observation of the teacher's behaviour management in a teacher directed group session (see Chapter 8);
- at least one observation of the teacher's behaviour management in a child-led session (see Chapter 8);
- at least one observation of the teacher's behaviour management in the outdoor classroom (see Chapter 8);
- a focused observation of arrival and departure times and of the changeover time for part-time children – this not only introduces routines but also gives you models of how experienced staff interact with parents;
- focused observation of fruit or drinks times;
- focused observation of story or action rhyme times.

MINI CASE MINI CASE MINI CASE **MINI CASE** MINI CASE MINI CASE **MINI CASE**

On my first placement I did some observation on my pre-placement serial days. I spent four days watching and helping groups. It meant I had seen most of a week and I had a feel for the rhythm of the class and expectations of behaviour. But I felt a bit of a fraud and I was really keen to get on to the teaching. I only had a four week placement, after all. I started teaching as soon as the placement began and built up to doing whole days in my second week. Looking back, I realise I didn't observe carefully enough at the beginning and now I wish I'd grabbed the opportunity when I had it. As the placement went on, I kept coming up with quite obvious questions about things like rules and routines that I should have been able to answer. I will be taking the observation part of the placement much more seriously on this placement.

Ann, PGDE

MINI CASE MINI CASE MINI CASE **MINI CASE** MINI CASE MINI CASE **MINI CASE**

As I had worked in the school for a year as a classroom assistant, I really didn't think I needed to do the observation tasks but my mentor was playing it by the book and made me use observation grids for lessons. It turned out to be really useful, particularly the observation for behaviour management. I found that when I took the class I was actually copying phrases and gestures the teacher used. I don't do that now, but it got me started and established me as a teacher. If I had to offer advice it would be to observe more than one teacher and see how different teachers implement the same policy.

Ellie, BEd

MINI CASE MINI CASE MINI CASE **MINI CASE** MINI CASE MINI CASE **MINI CASE**

My final placement was the really important one, because the way my course worked that was the assessed placement. I made sure I did the observations I needed. At the start of the placement I did routine observations of the teacher to learn how to manage the class. I also observed every subject before I taught it for the first time. As the placement progressed I used observations to address standards I still had outstanding. I did a really good afternoon observing the EAL teacher when she worked with some children in a group and some in a class. The strategies she used had been discussed in my course, but having the opportunity to see them used brought them alive and gave me ideas for using them in my class. It is hard to observe, because you feel you should be teaching but, as I see it, I might not get the chance when I am a probationary teacher.

Jo, PGDE

Focused observations

As your placement progresses, you will be able to select your observations in a much more purposeful way. You might observe your teacher for the following reasons:

- You have not had a chance to see a particular type of lesson. You will not want to wait three weeks before beginning your teaching and some subjects will be blocked so that they do not happen every week, or even every term.
- You have found a particular difficulty in your teaching and you want to find out how the teacher

addresses this (and develop your own confidence). For example, if you are unsure about how to use your voice to gain children's attention or you need some strategies for teaching phonics.

- You have an outstanding target to address and observation is the best way of doing this. For instance, if you are aiming to improve your differentiation through questioning, first see how the teacher does it.

To make the best possible use of these observations of your teacher's practice, make sure you have read any relevant documentation and are well prepared. If you are observing science, you will learn much more if you have read the school science policy and have looked at the relevant part of the curriculum for science. If you have been able to see the planning for the lesson you will learn even more.

In your placement you will also observe and talk to other teachers in your school because they are a huge resource of expertise.

- If you are in an Early Years setting you will observe the other members of the team, as the teaching of the group is a shared responsibility.
- If you do not have a chance to observe a particular type of teaching in your class your mentor can always arrange for you to go to another class. For instance, if your P2 class are doing art but not D&T this term, you can go to another class to observe D&T.
- If another class has a particular resource you want to see in use, such as an interactive whiteboard (IWB), parachute or outdoor area, your mentor may help you arrange an observation.
- If another teacher in the school has a particular expertise your mentor may well arrange for you to observe them teaching in this area, for instance a leading English or mathematics teacher or an ICT co-ordinator.
- Observing an additional support teacher is very valuable because you can gain insight into the processes of the ASL code of practice and also see teaching strategies at work.
- Observing an EAL teacher or support assistant will not only help you to understand a wide range of strategies, it will also help you to include them in your teaching.
- Observing a class outside your current stage will help you to understand the experiences and needs of children in the stage preceding and following years. It will help you to think about the demands of transition.

You need to be prepared to make the most of these observations. If you are going to observe the use of an IWB, review the notes of any training you have had so far. If you are going to talk to the additional support teacher and observe a group session, make sure you have read the school ASL policy and the IEPs of any children in your class.

Through observation you will learn that there are many different ways to be a successful teacher. On the basis of what you observe, you can start to develop a range of successful strategies. Once you use these strategies yourself they will become part of your personal teaching style.

Sample lesson observation format for Primary Classes

The purpose of observing experienced teachers is to examine the range of techniques that the teacher is using in order to reflect on your own practice. You can use this grid to make notes.

Trainee's name	Teacher observed	Date and time
Class	Lesson topic	
Starting the lesson/transitions within the lesson	Links made to previous learning	
Teaching strategies	Pupil activities	
Organisation of the learning	Use of resources (including use of ICT)	
Management of pupils	Strategies for assessing pupil learning	
Consideration of special needs	Teacher presence in the classroom	
Summarising and extending the learning	Concluding the lesson	

Sample lesson observation format for Early Years or Infant settings

Description of the area of provision (e.g. water/small world/role-play area)

Information about the children involved (e.g. number, age, sex. Is this a new activity for the children or one the children are very familiar with?)

Focus of the activity

What does the practitioner say and do?	What do the children say and do?

How does the practitioner monitor the children's achievements? How are children given feedback on their achievements?

Additional information, e.g. How long did the activity last? What did the children do next? What did the practitioner do next?

Planning and differentiation

There is no such thing as a good teacher who cannot plan well. Planning is the basis of good teaching and you have a number of reasons for becoming good at planning. First of all, you have to demonstrate that you meet the standards for ITE.

Section 2, Professional Skills and Abilities, requires teachers to meet the following elements for planning.

- 2.1.1 – Plan coherent, progressive teaching programmes which match their pupils' needs and abilities and justify what they teach.

- 2.1.3 – Employ a range of teaching strategies and justify their approach.
- Set expectations and a pace of work that makes appropriate demands on all pupils.
- 2.1.5 – Work effectively in co-operation with other professionals, staff and parents in order to promote learning.

To demonstrate these standards you will build your expertise at planning gradually as you progress through your placements.

The theory of planning is relatively straightforward and by the time you arrive for your placement you should know about some of the factors shaping the choice of what children learn and how they learn it.

A Curriculum for Excellence, 5–14 Guidelines,
Curriculum Framework 3–5
National Priorities

Local Authority guidance and policies and schemes of work

School policies and school targets

Medium-term planning and class targets

Each child's individual needs on the basis of previous assessments and individual education targets (IEPs)

Weekly planning

Previous lesson or daily planning

Your lesson

- The 'National Priorities In Education', as approved by the Scottish Parliament in December 2000, are defined under the following headings.
  - Achievement and Attainment
  - Framework for Learning
  - Inclusion and Equality
  - Values and Citizenship
  - Learning for Life.
- The rights of children and young people as set out in 'Safe and Well' (2005) which provides a set of standards protecting children and young people in relation to:
  - emotional, physical and mental health;
  - protection from harm and neglect.
- The 5–14 Curriculum Guidelines being replaced by A Curriculum for Excellence provides much of the content of the curriculum.
- The Curriculum Framework 3–5 and A Curriculum for Excellence provide the curriculum guidance for Early Years. The 3–5 framework gives 5 key aspects of children's development and learning in place of a curriculum.
  - Emotional, personal and social development
  - Communication and language

- Knowledge and understanding of the world
- Expressive and aesthetic development
- Physical development and movement.
- Local authorities will offer guidance about teaching and have requirements and policies for the curriculum. These and the school's policies and targets will also shape the material planned for lessons.
- Within school the curriculum co-ordinators will monitor plans and ensure the curriculum is addressed progressively and continuously.

You need to be involved in different levels of planning during your training. You will have to demonstrate that you know about medium-term planning, especially for language, mathematics, science and ICT for P1 to 7, or all five key aspects of learning for Early Years.

Medium-term planning

Drawing up a medium-term plan for, say, a half term, means dividing up the learning for the half term so that it can be taught in a continuous, progressive way that meets the needs of all the learners in the class. This is not as simple as it sounds. To do it you need:

- good knowledge of the curriculum documents (A Curriculum for Excellence; 5–14 Curriculum Guidelines; 3–5 Curriculum Framework);
- good subject knowledge so that you can make sensible divisions and links between elements of knowledge and skill;
- an understanding of how you will teach the subjects and what the pupils' likely responses will be;
- some experience or knowledge of how long it will take for children to learn each element of your plan.

These require some experience, so medium-term planning is usually the first type of planning you see but the last type of planning you actually do.

You may find it difficult to obtain experience of medium-term planning on your placements because teachers in school do this sort of planning well in advance and often refer to last year's plans. Also teachers may not work individually on medium-term planning but do it in planning teams involving all the teachers teaching the same year group or stage. It is quite usual for curriculum co-ordinators to work with planning teams or check their plans for a particular subject to ensure that the curriculum for that subject is covered effectively.

Medium-term plans are usually expressed in terms of broad objectives for what the children should learn and these are specifically referenced to (or copied from) the national curriculum programmes of study, schemes of work for early years and guidance on RE, PSHE and citizenship. To demonstrate that you know about medium-term planning you should meet with your teacher specifically to discuss planning using the guidance suggested in the practical task below. You can see exemplar medium-term plans for a variety of subjects on the LTS site (www.ltscotland.org.uk). If you have the opportunity to attend a medium-term planning meeting, even if it is not for a term when you will be on placement, you should seize the chance as it will give you the best possible training. This is an opportunity your mentor may be able to arrange for you.

Weekly or unit planning

A weekly plan, or plan for a sequence of lessons over a longer period, is constructed from the medium-term plan. It is more specific than a medium-term plan and may include not only the learning objectives but also the teaching activities, resources and assessment points of the lessons in the sequence. Teachers will usually have a weekly plan for each subject in P1 to P7, although there will often be strong links across the curriculum.

In the Early Years setting the plan for a week, or unit of work, will usually be written by the teacher. It may involve a larger team in a nursery setting. It will address all the areas of development and will usually be planned around a theme such as summer, the seaside, diwali, growing, myself, etc. This is to emphasise the links between different areas of development and ensure the learning makes sense to very young children.

There is no one correct format for weekly or unit plans. Most schools have at least one set format that they use for planning but many have different formats for different key stages or even different formats for different subjects. This is especially true in the case of language and mathematics in the Primary Stages, where the structures of the lessons may demand different planning grids. Weekly plans will be referenced to the relevant curriculum documents and will break down learning and teaching so that children can achieve the learning outcomes. This is a difficult skill because, as well as everything necessary for medium-term planning, you need to know:

- what children have already done, know and can do;
- the likely response of children to what you are planning;
- the pace at which children can work;
- any individual needs that demand differentiation at a weekly planning level.

Example forms for planning a sequence of lessons

Experienced teachers in some schools will teach from their weekly or unit plans. At the start of each placement you will not be able, or ready, to do this but you will use the teacher's weekly plans right from the start as guidance so that you know what to expect from lessons or sessions you are observing. By looking at weekly plans you can at least be sure what the learning objective of the lesson is and how you should support children in achieving it. When you start teaching you will plan your early lessons and parts of lessons on the basis of the teacher's weekly plans.

As your placement progresses, you will be required to write weekly plans (or sequences of lesson plans) for core subjects if you are a Primary trainee or across the five areas of learning in the 3–6 curriculum if you are an Early Years trainee. This does not mean that you will have to do this unsupported. You will seek careful advice about your first weekly plan and use the teacher's medium-term plans as a basis for writing weekly plans. If weekly planning is done as a year group, setting or phase team activity you will be able to do your weekly planning this way but you will be expected to make a significant contribution and to lead the planning at this level before you can achieve the Standards for ITE.

Sequence of lessons Term/Year Teaching group

(This derives from the school's medium-term plans)

Curriculum subject/Theme/Area(s) of learning

Broad learning outcomes (5–14/ACE)	Focused learning outcomes Attitudes, skills, knowledge and understanding	Key activities	Resources	Cross-curricular aspects	Planned method of assessment
Broad learning outcomes	**Learning outcomes** stating anticipated achievement in one or more of the following: • attitudes (show...) • skills (be able to...) • knowledge (know that...) • understanding (develop concept of...) These form the basis of assessment and are judged through planned outcomes.	**Activities** should: • enable learning outcomes to be met • include a variety of experiences that progressively develop children's learning • recognise pupils' diverse needs. (including pupils with ASL needs, gifted and talented pupils, and pupils with EAL) • take account of pupils' gender and ethnicity	**Resources** should be: • influenced by learning outcomes • listed in detail • considered with health and safety in mind • related to displays where relevant	**Opportunities** to develop significant and planned attitudes, skills, knowledge and understanding across the curriculum in (e.g.): • language • ICT • PSHE/Citizenship • other subjects/areas of learning where significant	**Anticipated evidence** • to demonstrate achievement of learning outcomes, and to inform assessment and record keeping (may be observational, verbal, written or graphic evidence, depending on activity) • to reflect a range of assessment methods

Sequence of lessons **Term/Year** **Teaching group**

(This derives from the school's medium-term plans)

Curriculum subject/Theme/Area(s) of learning

Broad learning outcomes	Focused learning outcomes	Key activities	Resources	Cross-curricular aspects	Planned method of assessment
Broad learning outcomes	Learning outcomes	Activities	Resources	Opportunities	Anticipated evidence

PRACTICAL TASK PRACTICAL TASK PRACTICAL TASK PRACTICAL TASK PRACTICAL TASK

Obtain your teacher's medium-term plans as soon as possible (usually on placement preparation days). Examine them carefully and ensure you know the following.

- What period of time does each part of the plan cover? What period of time does the plan cover in total?
- For P1 to P7 which parts of ACfE or 5–14 does this medium-term plan address? Make sure you look up all these elements and read them in detail because you do need to demonstrate familiarity with these documents.
- For Early Years settings, what literacy and mathematics outcomes and areas of learning and development does this medium-term plan address? Make sure you look up all these elements and read them in detail because you do need to demonstrate familiarity with these documents.

This part of the task will take you at least an hour or so and should be done before you go on to the weekly plan.

Ask your teacher for his or her weekly plans for one of the weeks included in the medium-term plan. Ensure you can answer the following.

- Which parts of the medium-term plan does the weekly plan address?
- Which parts of the relevant curriculum documents does this refer to? (You will be able to see this if you have done the first part of the task well.)
- How long will each lesson or session in the weekly plan be?
- What additional detail does a weekly plan contain that a medium-term plan does not?

If you are on placement in P1 to P7, you can now focus on one part of the weekly plan, perhaps mathematics, or science. If you are in Early Years setting you need to look at all the areas of learning.

- What resources are needed for the lessons in the weekly plan?
- Who will be teaching the lessons in the weekly plan? Are they for a particular set or area of learning?

Discuss your chosen element of weekly planning with your teacher. You should ask:

- How do you derive a weekly plan from the medium-term plan?
- What do you do if the children do not make the predicted learning gains in one week?
- How do you ensure that the learning is accessible to all the children in the class?
- How do you differentiate for children who have SEN, EAL or are more able?
- Please can you show me how you include children with IEPs or targets?

Lesson or session planning

A lesson or session plan is written from a weekly (or longer-term) plan. It is a detailed document that addresses every element of the lesson/session. For you this has two main purposes.

First, a lesson plan enables you to demonstrate that you can select the appropriate objectives, teaching methods, assessment points and resources to teach an interesting, relevant and successful lesson. Lesson plans serve to show you can identify children's learning and to lead on to the next teaching experience. Secondly, writing lesson plans is a formative experience that gives you the chance to rehearse lessons before you do them. In this way you learn to deliver the content you mean to deliver. You also learn to manage challenging aspects of teaching such as pace, questioning, class management and enthusiasm. By planning lessons carefully in writing, you will gradually develop the mental scripts for teaching, assessment and class management that experienced teachers have so that, eventually, you no longer need to write lesson plans. At the beginning of every placement you will be expected to write lesson/session plans for every lesson or session you teach but later in the placement your mentor may suggest you no longer need to do this. If this happens you may teach from weekly plans.

There is no perfect lesson plan format but lesson plans need to include most of the following.

- Class/group taught.
- Time and duration of lesson.
- Learning outcome(s). This is the most important point on the plan. What do you want the children to learn, understand or do as a result of your lesson? Think very carefully about expressing lesson objectives so that they are reasonable and achievable. A single session or lesson may address or contribute to a literacy or mathematics objective or to an early years area of learning but no lesson will cover one of these big objectives. You may want to reference them on your lesson plan but phrase your lesson outcome accurately so that the children can achieve it.
- Reference to the relevant curriculum documentation (5–14, ACfE, schemes of work, etc.).
- The structure of the session. Does the lesson have a three-part structure? Most lessons have an introduction, main body and a plenary. A mathematics lesson might have a mental/oral starter, a main activity and a plenary. An English lesson might have a shared part, a main activity and a plenary. In Early Years is there a teacher-led then child-selected activity? Do nursery children do a plan/do/review format?
- The timings of each part of the lesson.
- Key vocabulary to be used.
- Key questions to be asked.
- Key teaching points.
- Role of the teacher and classroom assistants.
- Learning activity (what the children do).
- List of resources and use of outdoor classroom (for early years stages).
- Identified outcomes (how will you assess whether the children have achieved their learning outcome?).
- Note of pupils' previous experience.
- Cross-curricular links.
- Use of ICT.
- Identified health and safety issues (such as glue guns, the need to wear coats, etc.).
- An evaluation section.

Here are some examples of lesson plans and formats. No format is perfect but any of these can be adapted and changed. Initially you will probably be given a set format to use. Your mentor will certainly, at some point in the placement, suggest that you adapt your lesson plan format to help you address a particular target.

- If you are finding it difficult to maintain the pace of a lesson, you may want to plan in five minute intervals and note down the times at the side of your lesson plans.
- If you are having difficulty focusing on key vocabulary, you may want to highlight or embolden this in your plan.
- If preparation is a particular target, you may need to list resources especially carefully.
- If moving the children around the classroom is an issue for you, you may want to plan transitions very carefully.

Your lesson plans could well change format for a short time to assist you in addressing your target.

Generic lesson plan to adapt for specific subjects (P1–P7)

Date	Class/year group or set including number of pupils
Pupils' previous experience	
Notes from previous lesson including errors and misconceptions that need to addressed in this lesson	
5–14, ACfE references including, where appropriate, level strand target, and skills and the school's scheme of work	Learning outcomes
Cross-curricular focus	
Resources for each phase of the lesson	Subject-specific language

Specific expectations for behaviour (make clear to pupils)

Appropriate speaking and listening outcomes. Planned links, where appropriate, to language, mathematics and ICT for all subjects.

Mental/oral starter/shared reading or writing or other introductory activity (Time)

Assessment

Activity and questions to ask   Can the pupils?

Introduction to the main activity (Time)	
Teacher	Pupils

Main activity (Time) Phase	Low attainers	Middle attainers	High attainers
Assessment Can the pupils?	Extension/challenge	Extension/challenge	Extension/challenge

Teacher's role during the main activity	
Differentiation/target-setting including IEPs where appropriate	Use of in-class support, including guidance to supporting adult(s)

Plenary (Time)

Key questions to ask/areas to discuss

Introduce homework where appropriate

Note any errors/misconceptions to focus on in the next lesson on this area.

Evaluation of the lesson
Annotate the plan, using a different colour. Add other working notes here. After the session make any relevant notes that will help you to support pupils' progression/plan a similar session. This may include references to specific pupils (which may or may not need to go on their records) /ideas to reinforce the learning/suggestions for alternative organisational strategies/comments on the appropriateness of the resources.

Focus on pupils' learning	
Pupils not reaching the objectives, how and why?	Pupils exceeding reaching the objectives, how and why?

Notes for next lesson focusing on teaching	
Good aspects of teaching	Areas for development

Generic lesson plan to adapt for Early Years Stage areas of learning

Focus of the activity
Children involved (e.g. number, age, sex. Is this a new activity for the children or one the children are very familiar with?) Self-selection? Practitioner-directed?
Resources/Description of the area of provision (e.g. water/small world/role-play area)

Key practitioner vocabulary and questions?	What do the children say and do?
Evidence of achievement	Interaction with others?
Observations of participants	Action for future activity

Your very first plans

Your very first plans on a placement will probably not be for whole lessons or sessions. Initially, you will plan for short parts of lessons or sessions such as the mental/oral starter in a mathematics lesson, a guided reading session for a small group of children, supervision of an outdoor activity or a whole class phonics game. In planning these parts of lessons you will have the chance to pay attention to detail and really concentrate on some important aspects of using plans such as:

- ensuring you say what you plan to say;
- maintaining a pace that is brisk and engaging but not so fast that the children are lost;
- questioning and interactive teaching.

Planning parts of lessons and teaching them is a good start to building up responsibility for whole lessons. Initially, you will want to ask your teacher to look at your plans and make suggestions. In this way you are more likely to pitch the activity at the right level for the children. This is a skilled exercise that demands some experience of the children and their previous work. When going into a new class you will need the support of the class teacher to pitch the level of the activities right.

Planner for a mental/oral starter

Date		Group/class		
Duration		5–14, ACfE reference		
Resources		Mathematical, literacy, etc., language		
Activity				
Questions				
Less confident		Confident		More confident
Assessment				
Less confident		Confident		More confident
Evaluation				

Planning for other adults in the class or setting

As your placement progresses, you will develop expertise and speed in your planning. You will plan for a wider range of subjects and a wider range of situations. One key issue you need to consider, as you assume a greater role in planning for the class and as soon as you are planning whole class lessons, is planning for classroom assistants. It is usual for teachers to teach with classroom assistants and to plan for them.

A planning format for a classroom assistant

Date...................................... Lesson focus..

Activity (a brief account of the activity and the CA's role in any whole class introduction, shared reading, mental and oral, etc.)
Equipment needed
Key vocabulary to use
Key questions to use
Notes

In Early years settings, nursery practitioners will have been trained and achieved at least an appropriate NC or NQ. They will probably use the same planning sheets as the teacher and will make evaluations and assessments like the teacher. Classroom assistants in primary classes may not have any formal qualifications for the post although some will be well qualified.

To ensure you work well with the classroom assistant and any other adults such as those working with children who need additional support for learning, you will need to plan their role in your lessons. It is not usual to provide them with written instructions but for some lessons you might like to use a set format to present clear instructions. Classroom assistants do not usually provide written assessments and should not be asked to assess children but they will usually give an oral report on the children's achievements.

Frequently asked questions

1 'I have been planning my lessons on the computer every night. It is taking me hours and hours to type them up and I am becoming very tired. What can I do?'

Your priority is clear, accessible, useful plans and it does not matter whether they are written or word processed. If writing by hand works better for you, then write the plans by hand. If it worries you, you can always word process plans for the sessions when your mentor or course tutor is observing you. This has the added bonus of showing that you are making an effort to assist the observer and you will gain points for taking a professional approach. Of course, you may find that the computer is faster if you are adapting Internet plans or using the same elements in different lessons.

2 'I have found loads of plans on the internet but my teacher says I can't just print these off and use them. Why not?'

There are hundreds of lesson plans available on sites like the Standards site (DfES), the Hamilton Trust site, the Primary Strategy site, etc. There is nothing wrong with these plans except that they are not necessarily right for your situation. To use them you must adapt them to the needs and prior experience of your children as well as the weekly or medium-term planning for your class. Once a unit of work is started, each group of children will work through at a different rate and no plans created at a distance can accommodate this. If you can adapt plans from the internet to meet the needs of your children and the pace of your planning, they may work very well for you. Most trainees use adapted, internet-based plans some of the time but many say they find it is just as quick to start from scratch. However, you cannot have too many ideas and Internet plans are ideal for generating ideas.

3 'I am on placement in an Early Years pre 5 unit and the staff are used to planning together as a team on a weekly basis. Each member of staff plans one or two areas of the curriculum. How can I get involved and get the right experience?'

This is a common situation and your mentor will have ways to involve you. You might start by creating more detailed session plans from the team's weekly plans for each area of learning you work in. This will help you to focus on the details of sessions such as key language, interaction with children and observation. As the placement progresses you will take a larger role in planning meetings and by the end of your placement you should be able to make helpful suggestions towards the weekly plan. Remember to do (and plan) the routine aspects of teaching at Early Years Stage that the team may not plan. These include reading to children regularly, managing fruit time, helping children to change books and take home books and story sacks, managing the home time routine and welcome, and modelling writing. Plan these sessions carefully.

4 'I write my lesson plans out in proper sentences but my friend uses note form. Who is right?'

Probably both of you. If note form is quicker and still includes detail it is a good working compromise. You can write in more detail when you know the lesson plan will be the object of scrutiny, such as for an observation by your mentor.

Evaluation

Planning goes hand in hand with evaluation. To demonstrate element 2.4.3 of the Standard you need to be able to improve your performance through self-evaluation. This is discussed in more detail in the next chapter but cannot go unmentioned here. Evaluation means considering:

- how well the children achieved your objectives;
- how well you planned, taught and managed teaching in relation to your targets.

You will be required to include evaluations on most of your lesson plans and you will see spaces for these in the proformas above. Evaluations will usually be brief and will usually focus on two aspects: what you did and what the children learned.

If every time you taught a lesson you wrote a detailed critique of your performance as a teacher, linked to the standards, you would never have time to teach. Perhaps this is why some trainees start every evaluation they write with the dreaded sentence 'The lesson went well'. This is an ineffective evaluation because it tells the reader nothing except that the trainee survived to teach again. What went well? Does 'well' mean the children learned something?

It is much more useful to focus on particular aspects of your teaching to evaluate and improve. This is the role of the targets that are discussed in later chapters. For example, if you are really concentrating on managing the class, then you need to monitor how successful you are at managing behaviour, what strategies worked and what progress you are making. If you have this sort of evaluation for a series of lessons you can decide when you have achieved this target and when it is time to identify a new target.

When you begin planning and teaching you will probably be very keen to hear positive evaluations but less keen to hear advice on improvement. However, you should develop your ability to listen to advice and act on it. Your teacher will be in a good position to obtain a wide ranging view of your performance and will help you to evaluate in a critical but positive way.

When your evaluation comment identifies work to be done always say what you propose to do in response. The very best planning is the sort that clearly uses evidence from children's previous attainment and leads on to influence the planning and teaching of the next session or lesson. This sort of evidence may be the annotations to a lesson plan you make in response to previous evaluations.

Differentiation

In order to meet the diverse learning needs of pupils, teachers aim to teach the knowledge, skills and understanding in ways that suit their pupils' abilities – this is called differentiation. You demonstrate your ability to do this through your professional knowledge (Elements 1.1.1 and 1.1.2), planning (Element 2.1.1), and your teaching (Elements 2.1.3; 2.1.4 and 2.1.5). When planning, teachers should set high expectations and provide opportunities for all children to achieve including:

- boys and girls;
- children with special educational needs;
- children with disabilities;
- children from all social and cultural backgrounds;
- children of different ethnic groups including travellers, refugees and asylum seekers;
- children from diverse linguistic backgrounds.

Differentiation is represented in different forms in your planning, and involves the following.

- Presentation – planning to use a variety of media to present ideas, offering vocabulary or extra diagrams to those who need more support. Writing grids might be a form of presentation to help young writers who need extra support, where more confident writers do not have such support.

- Content – selecting appropriately so that there is content that suits most children with additional content available to some. This might mean some children completing six calculations where others complete ten.
- Resources – use resources that support pupils' needs such as writing frame, language master word banks or spellmaster machines for poor spellers. For children with EAL you might need to ensure that target vocabulary is available in a written form.
- Grouping – grouping pupils of similar ability for targeted support or pairing with a more able pupil, teaching assistant or language support teacher.
- Task – matching tasks to pupils' abilities. This can mean different tasks for different pupils. It is sometimes a good idea to offer different tasks that address the same objectives to different pupils so that they can achieve success.
- Support – offering additional adult or peer assistance, from a CA, language support teacher or more experienced child.
- Time – giving more or less time to complete a given task can make the task more suitable to the particular pupils.

As you develop your planning you will need to be sure to address the needs of all children. To do this you will plan different activities, support, resources, content, time and presentation so that all the children can achieve the learning objectives. Although this sounds simple it demands really good knowledge of the content, the children and a range of teaching strategies. At first you may well over- or underestimate what children know and can do. You will only achieve appropriate differentiation by working closely with the teacher so that you find out what strategies are available and which work for these children. Key resources will be CAs, language support staff and the IEPs written for children with special needs. All these should be planned into your lessons.

REFLECTIVE TASK
REFLECTIVE TASK

Review your early plans for:

- a whole class session;
- a group activity;
- an individual task to be used with a larger group or class of children.

Focus on your use of questioning in each of these situations.

How have you differentiated the task to meet the needs of individuals?

Ensure you have considered:

- who you will question;
- the function of the questions (bringing to mind knowledge, checking, keeping order, etc.);
- how you will phrase questions and what key vocabulary you will use;
- what sorts of answers you are looking for.

Questioning is a key area for differentiation.

A SUMMARY OF **KEY POINTS**

> Observation is the first step towards teaching. You will need to observe at the start of a placement and during the placement. Do not teach a subject you have not observed. Observation is also a tool for increasing your knowledge and experience. Choose your observations to meet your training needs.

> Planning is the foundation of good teaching and learning. Careful planning will help you to teach the right content, manage the class, maintain a good pace, give children feedback and assess learning.

> You will encounter medium-term planning for a half term, weekly planning and short-term, lesson or session planning.

> Begin planning small elements of sessions and build up to whole sessions. When you can plan lessons build up to sequences of lessons or core subject lessons.

> Planning is often done in teams. You will be planning with the support of your teacher and, possibly, a wider teaching team.

> Seize any opportunity to be involved in medium-term planning and to attend planning meetings.

> Differentiate your plans so that all children are included and plan for classroom assistants and other practitioners.

> Evaluation is your tool for ensuring learning takes place – in yourself and the children. Evaluate lessons and sequences of lessons.

Resources

The main website for support and advice in Scotland is the Learning and Teaching Scotland (LTS) site – http://www.ltscotland.org.uk/
Here you will find information on all aspects of curriculum and teaching including the 5–14 Curriculum Guidelines, A curriculum for Excellence and the Curriculum Framework for Children 3–5, specifically for Scottish teachers.

The Government hand book on Child Protection for Staff, Schools and Education Authorities is 'Safe and Well' available at http://www.scotland.gov.uk/Resource/Doc/57346/0016229.pdf

The Child Policy Information site – http://childpolicyinfo.childreninscotland.org.uk/ contains accessible, comprehensive and up-to-date policy information relating to children and young people in Scotland. The website also contains a comprehensive directory/ archive of developments since 2002.

National Priorities – http://www.nationalpriorities.org.uk/index.html This website offers support to schools and education authorities taking forward the implementation of the National Priorities in Education.

The TDA has an ITT professional resource network that addresses many aspects of multicultural and multilingual education: www.multiverse.ac.uk

The teacher support network www.teachernet.gov.uk has additional advice about planning and offers access to over 2000 lesson plans.

4
Learning to teach on placement

By the end of this chapter you should:

- **know how to build up your teaching on placement;**
- **know some of the features of interactive teaching;**
- **know how to set homework;**
- **recognise opportunities to play a wider role in school;**
- **understand the role of school-based tasks in building up your experience.**

Teaching

Surprisingly, many trainees find teaching a class or group is less challenging than planning and assessing. You can aim to demonstrate that you meet standards in two sections.

In Professional Knowledge and Understanding, you:

- have acquired a knowledge and understanding of the relevant areas of the curriculum;
- demonstrate that you have acquired the knowledge and understanding to fulfil your responsibilities in respect of cross-curricular themes;
- demonstrate that you have acquired a good working knowledge of the sector and your responsibilities within it.

In Teaching and Learning you:

- communicate effectively using a variety of media to stimulate pupils and achieve the objectives of lessons;
- employ a range of teaching strategies and can justify your approach;
- set expectations and a pace of work which make appropriate demands on all pupils.

To tackle this daunting list of standards you should aim to build up your teaching gradually. Start by planning and teaching small parts of lessons, based on the class teacher's plans and using strategies you have seen the teacher using. This might mean you start in a P1 class by planning and managing a small word activity or a dramatic play area and work to interact effectively with children who choose to do that activity. In a P2 class you might start out by doing a whole class mental/oral starter in mathematics or a shared reading session in language. Further up the school you might start by taking a group guided reading session or using the interactive whiteboard to introduce a whole-class main activity in mathematics or literacy.

You will move on to teaching complete lessons with the support of the teacher, who will help you to establish yourself as a teacher, to maintain a purposeful working environment and to teach the appropriate material. As you develop confidence, a suitable relationship with the children and a range of strategies for teaching, you will plan and teach a wide range of lessons or sessions, increasing the range of strategies for differentiation and ensuring all the children's needs are met. Eventually, you will plan and teach sequences of lessons that take the children through a process of learning about a topic or set of skills. This process of building up your level of responsibility and range of teaching techniques is different for each trainee because your experience is unique and each class of children is different. We asked seven probationary teachers for their top ten tips for beginner teachers and this is what they suggested.

Know what you are talking about

You must be absolutely clear about what you are teaching so that you can introduce the topic clearly to the children and understand and address their errors and misconceptions. No one else can do this for you and if you do not have the necessary subject knowledge you may teach the wrong content or be unable to help children. Always research your lessons so that you can demonstrate element 1.1.1 of the Standards and check the relevant curriculum documentation.

Prepare your resources well in advance

If you do not do this, something is bound to come up. As a trainee teacher it will be harder for you to locate resources or have them produced, because you do not know the system. If you leave organising your resources until just before a session things are certain to go wrong (the copier will jam, the cornflour will go missing or there will be no blue paint). You will become flustered and this will unsettle the children.

Put up your objectives and discuss them

If you just write up outcomes for children, the outcomes will become so much classroom wallpaper. If you just discuss outcomes, some children will forget them. If you write them up, hold them up and discuss what they mean, there is a good chance that both you and the children will understand them.

Explain very clearly

Explain then check whether the children have understood you. Every teacher will be able to tell you about times when they have not said what they meant and have been faced with baffled children. Most children will answer 'yes' to the question 'Do you understand what you have to do?' so avoid this question. Say: 'Tell me what you are going to do'. Occasionally, you will find that they do not know and this will usually be because you have missed out a vital point. Try using little cards with key words to remind yourself of the points you have to explain.

Act as if you know the rules, rewards and sanctions

This will give you confidence: if you act as if you do not know the rules you will lose credibility in the eyes of your class. Even the youngest child can spot someone who does not know what they are doing. If you are unsure, you can always ask a child but ask in a way that suggests confidence: 'Right, now show me where you keep your book. Well done!' is better than giving an indication that you do not know what to do.

Keep children moving and keep them involved

If your questioning involves a whole range of children and demands that they do something in response to questions, they are much more likely to engage with the activity. In the section on questioning (see page 59) there is more advice on this. Even a little movement can make an activity more memorable and purposeful for children. For instance, ask children to perform action rhymes, not just recite them. Get them to stand up and sit down as they answer a rapid-fire tables test. These are small, important things but they can have a surprisingly positive effect.

Keep up the pace

Pace the lesson so that you maintain the children's engagement and fit your plenary in. The plenary is a very important part of a session. Your can restate the teaching points, monitor who has understood and take the learning forward in a very brief plenary. Even in Early Years children learn from a brief reflection. Maintaining pace is a real challenge when you begin teaching.

Ham it up

Use your voice, body and other visual aids in an exaggerated way to generate enthusiasm, interest and motivation.

Get to know the children and their abilities quickly

This is a counsel of perfection and you will find it very challenging. However, the sooner you have a broad understanding of children's current abilities and past experience, the sooner your lessons will go smoothly. Most teachers and trainees experience, when working with a new class, lessons that turn out to be unexpectedly short or long. Until you know the class you are not able to match the work to the children's needs. Meanwhile, check with your teacher often and get him or her to check lesson plans.

Give prompt, balanced feedback

Whether this is about knowledge, skills or behaviour, the most important thing is that you notice and respond. Generally, a small, positive response such as a nod, smile or 'Well done' is all that is required. Do not praise effusively – this devalues the currency. Remember that the children who need the feedback most are often those who are least able to wait for it.

Do not panic – ever

You are in control for as long as you stay calm and are enjoying your work. If you panic you will lose control and find yourself acting unwisely.

Questioning and interactive teaching

Questioning and interactive teaching are vital aspects of Early Years or Primary teaching.

2.1.2 – demonstrate that you can communicate with pupils clearly and offer explanations in a stimulating manner, and demonstrate that you can question pupils effectively and respond to their questions and their contributions to discussions.

Interactive teaching involves a powerful set of strategies to ensure children learn in ways that suit them best. It is also a very powerful ally for behaviour management. Children who are interested, involved and engaged with an activity are easy to manage.

Questioning

Optimise the interaction between you and your pupils by ensuring that your questioning is as effective as possible. Questioning, either by the teacher or among the children, is a crucial part of introducing a topic and effective at the end of the lesson. It allows you to:

- identify what children already know;
- engage them in finding out more;
- explore misconceptions and errors;
- theorise aloud about new ideas;
- demonstrate new learning.

There are a number of types of questions:

- *closed* questions have one clear answer (e.g. 'How much is two add one?');
- *open* questions have open-ended answers (e.g. 'How does the cornflour feel?');
- *product* questions are designed to find the answer to a particular problem;
- *process* questions are meant to elicit procedures, processes and rules used to get the answers.

The mix of question types you use will depend on the objectives of the session. Your teaching is likely to be more effective if you use more open than closed questions, and more process than product questions. It is very easy to maintain a brisk pace with low-level closed questions but this does not ensure the best learning.

How long you wait for answers depends on the type of question asked. Allow three seconds or so for a lower level factual recall question, and 10–15 seconds for higher level questions (those requiring more sophisticated thinking skills). This will seem a very long wait indeed, but avoid the temptation to fill the space with talk. After the waiting time has passed you should prompt the children. If you ask a complex question requiring a lot of thought, allow children some time to work the answer out on their own – this is where talk partners or the use of small whiteboards are invaluable. You will sometimes want to ask specific individuals in a questioning session and this can be a valuable part of your differentiation or assessment.

Getting some children, especially shy children, to answer a question can be problematic. Give children plenty of experience of interactive lessons, and create a positive atmosphere in which the risks of a wrong answer are bearable. Children are more likely to be involved if they feel confident that a wrong response will not elicit criticism or ridicule from you or other children.

Prompting can be useful to help children answer questions. There are three kinds of prompts:

- *verbal* prompts: these include cues, reminders, instructions, tips, references to previous lessons, or giving part sentences for children to complete;
- *gestural* prompts: the teacher models the behaviour of children in order to pre-empt any mistake, e.g. by pointing to the object they want a child to use, or showing how to hold a pen correctly;
- *physical* prompts: these may be necessary among young learners, e.g., if the child cannot yet hold a crayon or form letters or numbers, you can take their hand and guide them.

Vary your acknowledgement of a child's response according to the confidence with which they gave it: a correct, quick and firm response must be acknowledged in a businesslike way (a nod or a gesture), although lower ability and less self-confident children may need more praise. When a child answers a question correctly but hesitantly, give them more explicit feedback to reassure them that the answer was correct and help them remember the correct response. If several of the children seem hesitant you may be asking questions that they do not understand and may need to backtrack to make sure they are with you.

There are two types of wrong answers – those due to carelessness or lack of effort, and those due to a lack of understanding or knowledge. In both cases you need to show that the answer is wrong in a businesslike way without resorting to personal criticism. If an answer shows carelessness or lack of effort, move on quickly to the next child – the denial of possible praise is the best response to a lazy answer. Where there is lack of understanding or knowledge, prompt the child by simplifying the question (perhaps breaking it into a series of small steps) or hinting. If this fails, look to the next respondent for the correct answer, rather than giving it yourself. If a child gives a partly right answer, first make clear the part that is correct and the part that is not, to avoid confusing the child or the class. Then prompt the child to correct the incorrect part of the answer. If this does not work, ask another child to correct or develop the part-answer.

PRACTICAL TASK PRACTICAL TASK PRACTICAL TASK PRACTICAL TASK PRACTICAL TASK

Focus on your questioning. A really simple practical task you can do with your teacher is to ask him or her to observe a session where you question a group of children. For each box the observer should tick the type of question you asked and whether you asked a boy or girl.

Question type	Sex of child asked
Open	Boy
Closed	Girl

Discuss the results of this and consider whether you need to monitor the balance of your questioning.

Interactive teaching

Interactive teaching is simply varying your teaching so that it engages the maximum number of children. Interactive teaching enables you to address children's learning through different sensory channels and to elicit responses from as many children as possible. This means you can make assessments of more children.

Teachers in schools are currently concerned that children learn through a number of sensory channels: visual, auditory and kinaesthetic. Traditionally, we teach relying heavily on the auditory channel by telling children and expecting them to listen. However, it has been suggested that teachers should use more visual learning (based on looking) and more active, kinaesthetic learning. This may suit both the learning style of some children and the different learning requirements of different tasks.

Whenever you are talking to or questioning a group of children, ensure that as many as possible are engaged with you, are responding and are active. Use:

- small whiteboards on which answers can be written;
- talk partners, where children discuss a proposition in pairs for 20 seconds before responding;
- phonic or number fans to indicate responses;
- picture sorting cards and artefacts that can be held up in response to questions.

These strategies not only allow you to see at a glance how a wider range of children respond but they give children response time and activity, as well as visual cues.

Also consider how you can make even the simplest activity more active. For instance:

- if you are teaching children to sing the alphabet, give each child a letter card and play 'stand up' so that they have to stand up when their letter name is sung;
- use large PE hoops for sorting activities rather than small ones;
- do active phonics games or action counting rhymes daily;
- when you ask children to identify something in a whole-class lesson, get them to come out and show the others on the whiteboard, interactive whiteboard or text;
- look for opportunities in the outdoor classroom – placing objects on a large alphabet mat is a much more engaging phonic activity than doing a worksheet;
- act out action rhymes rather than simply singing them;
- use active mathematics games for the mental/oral starter.

You can also make learning more visual by asking children to represent thoughts in a variety of different ways – mind maps, grids, arrangements of objects, collections of digital photos and PowerPoint shows.

Frequently asked questions

1 'On my second placement the teachers do not teach language in the way my first school did. The phonics is done separately and my teacher does not do shared reading.'

There are lots of different ways of addressing the teaching of language. You should make sure you understand the way phonics is addressed and take part in teaching it. It is vital that you learn to teach this element of language. You can do a check to see that all the elements of effective language teaching are being done. Ask your teacher how she or he ensures the children study a wide range of texts. The teacher may well want to do some shared reading. If you are still concerned, discuss this with your mentor, who will probably not be surprised.

2 'I have been observing and working with groups and my mentor wants me to teach the whole class. I am nervous. Help!'

It sounds as if you have reached a point where you need to take a deep breath, plan carefully and – have a go. It is vital to teach the whole class, if only for short bursts like the mental/oral or shared writing initially. If you cannot do this you cannot be a teacher. You should teach the whole class quite early in the placement because the longer you leave it, the harder it is to begin and the harder it is to establish your role in the minds of the children. Review your observations, plan your first attempts carefully and check plans with the teacher. Do not expect everything to be perfect first time.

3 'In my nursery class unit, I don't have the chance to teach the whole class at once. Is this a problem?'

No, your unit probably does not use this organisation for sound educational reasons. Discuss these with your teacher or mentor and try to understand why a whole class grouping is not helpful here.

4 'I did my first science lesson yesterday and it was a disaster. I couldn't keep my eyes on all the children and some were rude and noisy. This was a lesson plan from my course. What am I doing wrong? Will I ever recover?'

Move on – but do not forget the experience. This lesson sounds as if it was too ambitious either for you or for the class at this point in your career. Review what went wrong very carefully: too much going on at one time? Content not right for the class? No monitoring? Too many resources? You might want to review this with your mentor or teacher. Plan the next lesson to avoid the same mistakes. You could help yourself by asking the teacher to work with you in a CA role in your next lesson. Everyone has some poor lessons but you will learn from these as well as from the good ones.

Setting homework

Homework is not statutory in schools in Scotland and, indeed, its educational value is dubious in terms of the difference it makes to pupils' academic outcomes. However, it is a very important way of engaging parents in their children's education. It is also valuable in giving parents the opportunity to demonstrate solidarity and support for the school by encouraging and supporting the completion of homework. Homework may also help children to develop their independence, self organisation and responsibility.

To see how much homework children should have in your school, you need to look at the school policy. Recommendations suggest that even at the end of P7 children should not have more than 30 minutes of homework a day. This homework might consist of:

- taking books (or story sacks) home to read with parents or a sibling, a practice that has demonstrated benefits even where parents do not speak English;
- taking home mathematics games to play with family members;
- homework sheets containing simple, planned work that does not demand elaborate resources and that can be done with parents or siblings;
- asking children to research a particular topic;
- asking children to ask family members questions about a particular topic;
- regular learning of spellings or multiplication tables for tests.

All these count as homework in the Early Years.

Make sure you know the school routine for setting homework.

- When do children take it home?
- When does it come back?
- Is there any marking to be done? If so, what sort of response is required?
- Find out how schools establish expectations in their parents. Most schools will have handouts for parents about topics like using story sacks, reading with your child, learning spellings, etc. Many schools will organise parent workshops to introduce these ideas to parents.

When setting homework make sure you:

- give children a reasonable time to complete the work (they may not be able to do all it on the same day) but not so long that they forget it;
- explain homework clearly and ensure that any sheets are sent home with brief instructions for parents;
- ensure that homework does not need much in the way of resources, as parents may not be able to find them at short notice;
- establish a routine that children and parents will remember easily;
- set work that everyone has equal access to – you cannot expect parents to drop everything and rush off to the library and not everyone has a computer;
- praise children for doing homework – however poor the results the child has made an effort and shown commitment;
- have consistent, non-judgemental expectations of all children – if you have set the homework appropriately you should expect all children to achieve it, whatever their social situation;
- support children who repeatedly fail to do homework by discussing it carefully, ensuring they understand and, if all else fails, giving them time to do it in school.

Setting, managing and marking homework is a very small part of your training but it is something you can easily achieve and feel satisfied about.

Professional values and the wider life of the school

As part of the Standards for ITE, you will need to demonstrate that you –

- 1.2.2 have acquired a good working knowledge of the sector in which they teach and their professional responsibilities within it
- 2.1.5 can work effectively in co-operation with other professionals, staff and parents in order to promote learning

To look further at the responsibilities and professional standards for teachers we suggest you consult the General Teaching Council for Scotland website on www.gtcs.org.uk This sets out and discusses the values and professional responsibilities of teachers. On place-ment you will certainly encounter a range of opportunities to display these values.

Some features of school life are discussed in the early chapters of this book – punctuality, attendance at staff meetings and careful preparation. These demonstrate your commitment to your role as a teacher and mentors invariably mention these issues when writing reports about trainees' progress. However, you will have other opportunities to participate in the life of the school. Some of these will be low key, such as greeting parents at the beginning and end of the day and planning interesting displays of work. Others will be very high profile, such as being invited to go with the school on a residential trip to a study centre. Between these two extremes are all the events, routines and celebrations that are part of school life – sports day, Eid, Christmas, book week, the summer play, class assemblies and day trips. Although they may seem a demanding extra dimension on top of daily planning and teaching, these are the events that allow us to share our values and enthusiasms with children. These events are every bit as educative as the formal curriculum and will also promote key skills such as cooperation and flexibility.

You will need to seek out some opportunities. For instance, if you want to know about the work of the school board, you will need to do a little research on the Internet and then arrange a meeting with a school board member, through your mentor. If you are well prepared, you can find out all you need to know in this way.

Trainees often worry about whether they have done enough to address the standards relating to working with parents. You need to ensure you take opportunities to:

● observe your teacher (and others) interacting with parents on a daily basis at the beginning and end of school;
● greet parents yourself (when this is appropriate);
● observe at a parents' evening or open day;
● discuss with a teacher the school's efforts to involve parents;
● ask to look at the literature that goes home from school to parents, including advice about reading with children, spelling sheets and school newsletters or bulletins.

PRACTICAL TASK PRACTICAL TASK PRACTICAL TASK PRACTICAL TASK PRACTICAL TASK

Identify your opportunities to take a full professional role. Use the checklist below to identify what experiences you have already had (column 1) then use column 2 to identify some experiences to aim for in your next placement.

Opportunity	Experienced	Identified for next placement
In the classroom		
Attendance register		
School meal numbers		
Welcome parents and carers before and after school		
Deal with absence notes		
Manage the collection and marking of homework (books to read, etc.)		
Set homework		
Create a display in your class		
Create an interactive area in the setting		
Other		

Beyond the classroom		
Set out and use the gym or hall		
Teach in the ICT suite		
Teach on the field or playground		
Attend a staff meeting		
Attend planning meetings		
Attend a whole staff Inset session		
Participate in a parents' evening		
Attend a PTA event		
Participate in a school visit		
Attend a school board meeting or discuss it with a school board member		
Play a musical instrument in assembly		
Run, or participate in, a class assembly		
Participate in an after school club or coaching		
Take part in a school visit		
Attend sports day		
Participate in a transition visit to a secondary school		
Participate in a book, arts or charity day		
Attend the breakfast club		
Other		

School visits

To demonstrate you can plan for children to learn in out-of-school contexts (Element 2.2.1 – know how to make use of the environment and resources outside the school to support teaching and pupils' learning) you do not actually have to plan a visit to another setting. Ideally you would do so, working through the following checklist with your teacher. This might be a visit to a museum, gallery, supermarket, DIY store or local park. However if you cannot arrange a visit with your class, you should ensure that you use your placement to look at school and local authority policies and practice on school visits. In addition, take the opportunity to look at the wide range of information and advice available on the LTS website under 'Taking Learning Outdoors' at – http://www.ltscotland.org.uk/takinglearningoutdoors/index.-asp

Additional information can be found on the Health Promoting Schools site at http://www.healthpromotingschools.co.uk/practitioners/topics/physicalactivity/learningoutdoors.asp

Further advice on safety issues can be found at – http://www.scotland.gov.uk/Publications/2004/12/20444/48943

PRACTICAL TASK PRACTICAL TASK PRACTICAL TASK PRACTICAL TASK PRACTICAL TASK

Identify your opportunities to use a wide range of resources. Use the checklist below to identify what resources you have already used (column 1) then use column 2 to identify some resources you aim to use in your next placement.

Resources selected and used	Last placement	Next placement
Write on a flipchart or whiteboard		
Selected story or poetry		
Use an OHP		
Use a data projector		
Use an interactive whiteboard		
Use a TV programme		
Use a radio programme		
Use a tape recorder		
Use reprographic equipment		
Teach in an ICT suite		
Use ICT for preparation and planning		
Set out and use the gym or hall		
Use the outdoor classroom or field		
Other		

Checklist for out-of-school visits

Do you have information about?

School's policy on trips to include: • Adult/pupil ratio/supervision • Charging for school trips • Using transport for school trips • First aid/inhalers • Insurance in relation to school trips • Emergency procedures • Exploratory visit by trip leader
Risk assessment procedures
Information to pupils
LTS guidance on health and safety of pupils on educational visits
LA guidance on health and safety of pupils on educational visits
Letter/consent form proformas
Proposal form for HT outlining the objectives, cost, intended leaving/returning times and cost estimate
Schedule of trips planned for the year across the whole school
School's procedures on parents' information evenings/sessions in relation to school trips
Other guidance used in school
Useful contacts used by the school
Specific details of a trip already undertaken or to be taken in the current school year

Communication with parents and carers

As a trainee you will communicate with and report to parents to meet Elements 2.3.1 and 2.1.5, but you will do this under the supervision of your teacher and only in a limited way. This does not stop you from learning about the processes of communication in your setting. These might include any of the following:

• school newsletters;
• school-run reading or mathematics schemes;
• parent-run projects like story sack workshops;
• the daily communication of meeting parents delivering and collecting their children;
• home visits for those children starting in a new setting;
• parents coming into school to do a regular activity like cooking with children;

- parents or grandparents coming in to talk to pupils about a topic;
- routine parents' evenings or day workshops;
- written reports to parents.

Some of these opportunities are more readily available to you in certain placements. For instance, if you are placed in the Early Years setting you are almost certain to have the chance to meet parents or carers and talk to them at the beginning and end of the session. If you are in Upper Primary, you may only see parents at formal parents' evenings. If you are fortunate enough to be in school for parents' evenings or home visits you should ask to sit in. You will not usually have a real role in reporting but you will be able to observe the teacher at work. Writing reports for parents is a task you might practise at some time during your placement. Collect evidence of the attainment of a few children and write mock reports, using the school system. Guidance about communicating with parents is available on the LTS website as 'Parents as Partners in Learning'.

Completing school-based tasks

As part of your training you will almost certainly have a range of placement tasks that are an important part of your learning experience. These may be tasks arranged by your mentor to ensure you have appropriate learning experiences. They may be tasks connected to assignment or dissertations or they may be tasks set by your course tutors to contribute to your development and, possibly, your taught sessions. It would be easy to see these tasks as a distraction from the business of teaching but they do help to ensure you have the necessary range of experiences to meet the standards or to complete academic parts of your qualification. Never ignore these tasks nor leave planning them until the placement is well underway. Plan these tasks right at the beginning of the placement so that you can see what you have to do week by week, then build them into your timetable for the week. If you are undertaking school-based tasks or a research project in school there are some key points to think about at the start of the placement.

- Ensure you are totally clear about what school-based tasks or assignments you need to accomplish during the placement. Although other tasks may well be suggested as part of your training, those you start out with are essential. If you don't plan for them you won't accomplish them.
- Review the aims and scope of your tasks or project and ensure you can achieve them in the time available. Make sure, if you are addressing a particular research question, that you are clear how you will collect evidence. If you have school-based tasks, be clear about how much written evidence you need.
- Look at your course documentation or talk with your mentor to establish what proportion of time you should spend on your tasks or study. You can then negotiate appropriate times around your teaching commitments.
- Check that you are able to work with the resources or pupils you need. Sometimes school plans change suddenly and you may need to re-negotiate.
- Where there is background reading or research to do to prepare for your tasks or study, ensure you have done as much as possible before the placement. In this way your tasks will be well focused and you will waste less of your precious time.
- Check that any research you want to carry out with children or teachers in your school is ethical and professionally appropriate. Your university will have guidelines on this.
- Review your project or tasks and list the school staff you would like to talk to or observe. If you are ready with this list, you can discuss it with your mentor.

Some tasks will be routine teaching that you would do anyway, others may encourage you to focus on a particular aspect of the curriculum or a group of children. Consider each task carefully and be clear about what you will need to do to accomplish it.

For example, a task may require an in-depth look at a small group of pupils. Now is the time to ask yourself some questions.

- Have you identified this group?
- Are these pupils from your own class or will you need to identify pupils from another class or age group?
- Have you spoken to your mentor about arranging a visit to another class and to the teacher concerned?
- Do you know where the individual pupils fit into the academic range of the class?
- How much time is needed in order to carry out these tasks?
- Have you discussed them with your class teacher and school mentor?
- Have you planned time in which you can carry out these tasks?
- Once you have carried out the tasks, will you need to set aside time to complete any writing up?
- Consider whether you should share this information with anyone and how you will ensure it is confidential.

Discuss your school-based tasks with your mentor early on in your placement and monitor them at mentor meetings. This is a very good opportunity for you to demonstrate a professional, organised approach to your work. If you are planning and working through school-based tasks you appear very much more organised and competent than if you leave them until the last fortnight then panic.

If you are doing a project or study involving the children or teachers in your school you will have to make decisions about how far you share data you collect with the children or teachers. Whatever you decide, you should ensure that you have the full consent of all participants in any study and that you anonymise the names of pupils, teachers and schools in such a way that they cannot be identified in any report or dissertation.

REFLECTIVE TASK

Audit the range of:

- pupil groupings;
- resources;
- interactive learning strategies (questions, etc);

you have used on placement so far.

Complete the chart on page 70 with your examples.

Learning objective	Pupil grouping	Resources (including e-resources)	Interactive teaching/ learning strategies
	Whole class or group		Small whiteboards
	Individual pupil	Self-selected book	
	Ability group		
	Mixed ability group		

Which opportunities have you missed so far? When can you plan to try out a grouping or teaching strategy you have not used so far?

A SUMMARY OF **KEY POINTS**

> **Being well prepared and appearing confident are key factors in successful teaching.**

> **You should ask a range of question types and ensure you question a whole range of children. Questioning is a skilled business and you can practise and improve your questioning so that it is a useful differentiation tool.**

> **Interactive teaching means involving children actively in their learning. It can increase learning in whole-class and group settings. Placement is your chance to develop your use of interactive teaching.**

> **Homework is a term covering a wide range of activities. Get involved with whatever counts as homework and be thoughtful in setting work for children.**

> **Professional placement offers a wider range of opportunities for you to demonstrate your values and become involved in the school – seize these opportunities.**

> **Successful completion of school-based tasks depends on planning for their completion early in your placement.**

Resources

To look at the professional roles and responsibilities – www.gtcs.org.uk (Scotland)

All aspects of the curriculum can be found on the Learning Teaching Scotland website at www.ltscotland.org.uk

5

Learning to assess, monitor and report on children's progress

By the end of this chapter you should:

- **know the main types of assessment;**
- **know what assessment tasks you need to engage in;**
- **know the role of target-setting.**

Assessing and monitoring

This book summarises some key points about assessment. You need to demonstrate that you have professional knowledge and understanding about assessment, as set out in the benchmarks for ITE. You need to –

Under Education Systems and Professional Responsibilities –

- In 1.2.2 – know about reporting to parents and guardians on their children's progress and discussing matters related to their children's personal, social and emotional development in a sensitive and constructive way.

Under Teaching and Learning –

- In 2.1.3 – Demonstrate the ability to evaluate and justify the approaches taken to learning and teaching and their impact on pupils.

Under Pupil Assessment –

- The whole of 2.3.1 – Understand and apply the principles of assessment, recording and reporting.
- The whole of 2.3.2 – Use the results of assessment to evaluate and improve teaching and to improve standards of attainment.

You should know what the children can do, note what they have done and identify what they and you need to do next. It is also important to be able to share this information with parents, children and at a school and government level to measure individual, school and national progress. This is the role of assessment. The two main types of assessment you will encounter are *formative* and *summative*.

Formative assessment (assessment for learning, or AFL) is assessment that directly contributes to your teaching. Each time you teach a lesson you assess what the children have achieved relative to your objective. You then act on this by planning the next lesson to take account of how well the children achieved your objective. In Early Years setting, a great deal of observation is planned to assess how children are developing in the five areas of the curriculum. This is supplemented by work done by children and records of discussions with children.

Summative assessment (Assessment of Learning or AoL) is assessment that gives you a snapshot of the child's achievement at a particular time. It is particularly useful assessment for reporting to parents or to government.

In Scotland the obvious examples are National Assessments – assessment materials supplied by the SQA and used by teachers to support the other evidence they have for children's achievement such as day to day observations and work. The assessment is carried out when the teacher has decided that a child or group of children has achieved the next level in maths or language. The assessment results are reported to the children and parents and are analysed at Local Authority level.

In Early Years settings, teachers collect together all their evidence from formative assessment and make a summative judgement about a child's progress in the areas of learning. This is reported to the parents and used to write a profile of each child that is passed on to the relevant P1 teacher.

These are examples of summative assessment but the term also applies to class tests that the teacher might use at the end of a section of work.

Assessment is theoretically very simple but is extremely difficult to organise and manage in practice. There are only three things you can assess: what the children know, what they do and what they produce. The simplest ways to assess these things are to:

- ask children what they know and note what they say;
- observe what they do and make notes (or take photos);
- collect and annotate what they produce.

These are your sources of evidence. In practice it is rather trickier than this because teachers are trying to make balanced assessments of a huge range of skills, knowledge and understanding for all the children in the class. Managing this will always be a challenge. On placement there are a number of key assessment and recording experiences you should seek to have, although you might not have all of these in early placements.

Giving feedback and making assessments

Giving feedback and making assessments as you teach is vital and addresses Element 2.3.2. This sort of assessment should be part of your teaching from the outset. You need to be clear when giving feedback. Do not praise wrong answers. Indicate that they are wrong but do not dwell on them. Where an answer to a question is partially correct, emphasise the correct part. Where a child has an obvious misconception you need to explore this and find out why. Praise children often but not effusively so that praise is seen as a reward.

Recording attainment on your lesson plans

This is a basic type of assessment you can start right from the beginning of the placement. The key to this is identifying clear statements of what you are looking for in your lesson plans that will allow you to assess who achieved the objectives of the session (or lesson).

For example, in one particular lesson you may find that a large number of children found the objective too challenging. In response, you have to amend your next lesson to revisit some aspects of the earlier content. Alternatively, you may find that the objective was not challenging enough for some children and realise you have to provide more challenge for them in the next lesson. This is good teaching and a canny trainee will make quite sure that mentors can see that you do change your lesson plans in response to the outcomes of previous lessons. Some trainees deliberately highlight changes to lesson plans to emphasise that their responses to assessment are to do something in their teaching.

Recording the attainment of the whole group

This is the next step. To do this you can use a class or group grid, which will give you a very easy recording format but little detail. You can use a system of ticks or stars to show how well the outcome has been addressed. This format should be adapted as appropriate, with columns and headings to suit circumstances. Records should be dated, systematic, regularly updated, manageable and should clearly summarise learning and inform future teaching. Names of pupils may be arranged to reflect class groupings and should be confidential.

Comments on significant individual responses may also be evident in lesson/activity plan assessments and evaluations with points considered for the next lesson/activity.

Class/Group	Subject/Area of Learning ....
Names of Pupils	Experience and Achievement

Compiling a pupil profile

A pupil profile will give you an overview of an individual child and also show you just how much varied evidence you need to make judgements about performance. You may well be asked to do this for a number of pupils as a directed task on placement.

Pupil profile

Name of pupil ....   **Class** ....

This record is designed to reflect pupil progress during the placement:

- to contribute to the school's own pupil records;
- to provide evidence to support reporting to parents.

This record may be adapted to suit the balance of areas taught:

Subject	Comments *(dated entries to record key points in learning)*
Language	
Mathematics	
Science	
ICT	
PSHE/Citizenship	

RE	
D&T	
History	
Geography	
Art	
Music	
PE	

Key targets for pupil's development:

- **completed by end of school experience;**
- **based on evidence in profile above.**

Pupil profile (Early Years setting)

Name of pupil .... Class ....

This record is designed to reflect pupil progress during the placement:

- to contribute to the school's own pupil records or Early Years Profile;
- to provide evidence to support reporting to parents.

This record may be adapted to suit the balance of areas taught.

Area of learning	Comments *(dated entries to record progress in learning)*
Emotional, personal and social development	
Communication and language	
Expressive and creative development	
Knowledge and understanding of the world	
Physical development and movement	

Key targets for pupil's development:

- completed at end of school experience;
- based on evidence in profile.

Levelling children's work

Most teachers make assessments of the level at which children are working by comparing examples of their work against the targets and skill descriptors in the current curriculum guidance. For mathematics it might be an assessment at various stages in the programme of work for that level. In addition to samples of work, teachers regularly record their observations of and discussions with each child and include these observations and notes in their assessment of levels.

Observing the administration of National Assessments

This will be important whatever age phase you are teaching. The tests are used to provide a summative (or snapshot) assessment of the children's achievements. They are administered in maths and language (reading and writing) only. The tests are administered when a child is considered ready to move up to the next level. A child will be described as, for example, 'working at level B' which means they are working on the level B targets and skills. When ready, they will sit the level B test and if successful and the teacher's own judgment gauges them ready, they will move onto level C work. The system may change as a Curriculum for Excellence is developed.

The tests are downloaded from the SQA site by a designated member of staff and delivered following the set instructions. The tests are marked by the teacher following a set of strict criteria and reported back.

Since the tests are administered when the children are ready, it is likely that the class you are in will not be sitting tests when you are on placement. You might discuss with your mentor the possibility of observing testing in another class and the administration of testing with a designated member of staff.

Contributing to the Early Years Profile or school reports

Many schools are moving towards a variety of ways of reporting to parents rather than relying solely on the traditional 'parents' evening' and written report/s. Reporting to parents may now consist of a number elements including such things as their involvement in their child's personal learning plan; regular contact with class teachers; involvement in assessing and evaluating work brought home by their child; open days where they can come into classes during lesson time and see how their child is performing etc.

School reports are still an important element of the reporting system and you should try to find out the format used in your placement school. Most schools have a format that they use which may be common to all the schools in a particular authority or be individual to that school.

If you are able, it would be good practice to try writing some elements of a report for children in your class and scrutinise these with your mentor. Report writing is an area that will be focussed on in your probationary year where you will receive appropriate instruction and support writing the reports for your class.

Setting targets for children

During school experience you will also be expected to use your records of assessment to set realistic and demanding targets for your pupils.

You also need to be aware of government targets, e.g. in areas such as language and mathematics, as well as school targets based on a variety of data including schools' test scores in relationship to those of similar schools – *benchmarking*.

Setting targets in the classroom

When setting targets in the classroom, you should consider:

- school targets (obtain a copy of the relevant information);
- issues affecting the whole class (academic and non-academic);
- issues affecting groups within the class (academic and non-academic);
- issues affecting individuals within the class (academic and non-academic).

Consult your class teacher or mentor about these.

Setting targets for classroom improvement

When setting targets with pupils, the process already established for your own target-setting may be used, with minor changes. You will need to start with pupils' current knowledge, understanding, skills, behaviour patterns, etc. However, in place of the standards for ITE you will need to consider targets and policies already in place within the curriculum. The rest of the process follows the same route as your own target-setting.

The nature of target-setting with the whole class, groups and individual children varies. Some targets will be long-term and may feature school priorities that are in the challenging zone. You will almost certainly need to work through the planning cycle (Figure 5.1), record your plan and share it with all those involved. On other occasions, for example after marking pupils' work, it might be sufficient to agree a target in the comfort zone with the pupils and write it on the board or in the pupils' books.

In many schools, teachers work with individual pupils to set personal targets called a Personalised Learning Plan (PLP).

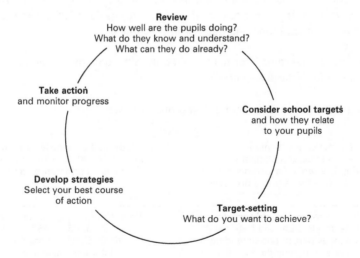

Figure 5.1. Target-setting as part of a cycle for improvement

Working with elements of the cycle

Reviewing

Before you set targets with your pupils you need to review with them their current performance in the area designated for improvement. Evidence relating to how well pupils are doing may be obtained from a variety of sources and used when setting individual, group or whole class targets. You might consider, where appropriate:

(a) pupils' exercise books, pictures or work folders;
(b) records of assessments made by you, your teacher and other practitioners;
(c) displays of pupils' work;
(d) comments made by the class teacher or other colleagues, including annotations on saved work giving the context and task;
(e) your own observations within and outside the classroom;
(f) the pupils' comments related to the proposed area for development;

When reviewing you should:

(a) use appropriate evidence of pupils' current performance;
(b) discuss the current situation with pupils and obtain their perspective. You could get them to carry out a simple self-evaluation.

Working with school targets

Schools and head teachers use evidence of attainment from pupil's work, results of National Assessments, teacher's judgement and moderation exercises with other schools within the local area as part of monitoring the establishment's progress and provision. They use this and other relevant information from self-evaluation using the HGIOS (How Good is our School) format to set appropriate targets for improvement.

Local authorities use the same information to report to the government and to set their own targets and those for individual schools.

The following format for assessment is being put into place –

	Formative	
Formative assessment Personal learning planning Involving learners, and parents and other adults, in the learning process		local authority collection and analysis of information to inform provision and improvement
Internal		External
Teachers' judgements and reports, with local moderation and National Assessment as part of understanding and sharing standards		Scottish Survey of Achievement P3, P5, P7, S2 National Qualifications (SQA) international studies HMIE inspections and reports on authorities and schools
	Summative	

Figure 5.2. Assessment format
(from Scottish Executive Circular No. 02 June 2005)

Teachers will take part in the self-evaluation process of the school and will have a role in meeting the targets set. This might mean target setting at the appropriate level for the class. Where the targets are long-term, it will be necessary to break them down into manageable steps.

You are not expected to know the full details of these targets but may discuss class targets with your teacher.

Target-setting

You may be asked to identify, with the pupils, clear and measurable targets that take them forward from their current performance. When schools set targets they are encouraged to think SMART: **s**pecific, **m**easurable, **a**chievable, **r**ealistic, **t**ime related.

As part of the Assessment is for Learning programme, many schools have introduced Personal Learning Plans, (PLP's) for each child. The plans are decided upon by consultation with the pupils individually and may include involvement of parents and support workers. The PLP follows a five stage cycle.

The five-stage personal planning cycle

For an individual learner, the self-evaluation and planning process has a series of supported stages.

1. REVIEWING CURRENT LEVEL OF DEVELOPMENT – including evidence of attainment, history of what works well (e.g. preferred learning styles and types of learning activities favoured).
2. TARGET-SETTING for the next block of learning – based on findings in Stage 1 (REVIEW).
3. PLANNING LEARNING ACTIVITIES – based on stage 2 (TARGET-SETTING) and stage 1 (REVIEW).
4. LEARNING – through PLANNED ACTIVITIES set out in Stage 3.
5. EVALUATING LEARNING AND PROGRESS – achievement at the end of the learning block, in relation to targets and learning activities.

Back to REVIEWING for the next block of learning.

An important feature of the PLP is the involvement of the pupil in the process. When setting targets in general, you should keep the following in mind:

• consider your review of pupils' work and pupil self-evaluation;
• consider school targets, class targets, etc.;
• write lesson/session/day targets (or learning outcomes) clearly on the board;
• make long-/medium-term class targets (e.g. rules) clearly visible and refer to them;
• make individuals' targets clearly visible, e.g. use a particular colour when you or they write targets in their books (some non-academic targets can be written on small cards and taped to the pupils' tables);
• communicate with parents on a daily basis, sharing the targets with the home and let parents know of successful achievements;
• make your targets:
  – SMART;
  – in the challenging as well as the comfort zone.

- make certain that the pupils have a clear picture in their minds of what success will look like. Get them to tell you what they understand to be a successful outcome. Check that it matches your criteria.

Developing strategies

You now need to think of ways to put your carefully framed targets into action. When developing strategies to improve pupils' performance, you may consult with mentors, tutors and other students, read appropriate articles and books, or brainstorm. However, when working with pupils you will mainly be discussing their targets with them. If possible let them make suggestions and thus acquire some ownership of the strategies about to be implemented. You must be careful to avoid dashing into action with your first idea without considering its implications or alternatives that might be more promising.

When developing strategies you should:

- consider a number of possible courses of action and include pupils in discussing them;
- select actions most likely to succeed;
- consider what support you will need to implement the plan;
- list any resources you will require to implement the plan;
- when necessary, have a timetable for implementing the various parts of the plan.

Taking action and monitoring progress

While implementing your strategies, you will need to check that you are on track by reviewing and monitoring progress made by the pupils. You may wish to enlist the help of the pupils in keeping records of their progress. In doing this you can be creative in designing, or encouraging pupils to design, appropriate recording sheets. You will find that some pupils will be used to discussing their progress and will be developing their understanding and language about this while others will have less experience and find it hard to monitor and discuss their progress. Even the youngest child in the Early Years setting can begin to plan, do and review what has been done and that reflection can be learned early on.

When monitoring progress you should:

(a) consider with the pupils their progress against the targets, using records as evidence;
(b) consider with the pupils progress in relation to the time scales;
(c) decide if you need to reconsider your strategies with the pupils;
(d) decide with the pupils if you need to modify the targets.

This is often done as part of a Personalised Learning Plan.

Actively involving children

When working with children you should try to increase motivation by giving them some ownership of the target-setting, monitoring and recording processes. Celebrate children's success. How does the school do this – awards, certificates, stickers, displays, etc.? Discuss this with teachers, mentors and children. You can set and celebrate targets in many aspects of school life. Be creative.

Always be aware of the importance of recognising success when pupils achieve their targets. This reinforces desirable behaviour patterns, helps to develop self-esteem and encourages even greater effort. Children's achievements need to be recognised across the curriculum and opportunities for success must be provided. Work needs to be differentiated so that it is set at an appropriate level and there is also the element of challenge. This enables children to strive for and achieve success (see Figure 5.3).

REFLECTIVE TASK

Plan a discussion with the assessment co-ordinator in your school. Ask some of the following questions:

- What are the school improvement targets?
- How were these targets identified?
- Who has been involved in addressing these targets?

Then consider how the school targets are reflected in the curricular planning for your class.

Appropriate and challenging work

Striving to reach attainable goals

Successful experience

Developing confidence and self esteem

Further motivation

Figure 5.3. Achieving success

A SUMMARY OF **KEY POINTS**

> Assessment and monitoring of pupil performance begins with clear planning. Ensure your assessment criteria are included in your plans and evaluate them.

> Assessment, planning, target-setting and teaching are processes in a cycle that generates learning and school improvement.

> Schools, classes and pupils will all be working with targets for improvement and you need to know what these are.

> You will need to discuss target-setting in school with your teacher or mentor at two levels – whole-school targets and how your class are addressing these; and targets for individuals and groups in the class.

> There are key assessment experiences you should have at some time in your placements. These include routine evaluations and record keeping, levelling of children's work in various curriculum areas, completion of pupil profiles, completion of school reports, contribution to the Early Years Profile and observation of statutory tasks and tests.

Resources

Details of government consultations and policy on assessment can be found on the Scottish Government site http://www.scotland.gov.uk/Home

LTS has a section on Assessment is for Learning with links to parental involvement and personal learning plans at – http://www.ltscotland.org.uk/assess/index.asp

Scottish Executive Circular No. 02 June available from http://www.scotland.gov.uk/Resource/Doc/54357/0013630pdf.

The Scottish Qualification Authority (SQA) site is the location of the Assessment Materials at http://www.sqa.org.uk/sqa/1.html

6

Individualised training: target-setting, observation and assessment on placement

Teaching placement is different for every trainee. You have a unique background and experience and each class you encounter is different. In this section we examine key issues for you as a trainee – how your placement is shaped, directed, monitored and assessed. You need to understand these processes to use them purposefully.

By the end of this chapter you will:

- **know what to expect when you are observed;**
- **understand the role of target-setting in your professional development and how to set targets;**
- **know how to prepare for, conduct and follow up mentor meetings;**
- **be able to manage and prepare for your assessment against the standards for the award of provisional registration;**
- **recognise the link between your placement and your professional development as a probationary teacher.**

Observation

One of the most useful experiences you can expect to have as part of your training is to be observed teaching. It is also one of the most realistic professional experiences you will have because teachers are observed throughout their careers. You will see that teachers in your placement schools observe each other, are observed by subject co-ordinators, head teachers, local authority advisers and HMIE inspectors.

During your initial teacher training you may be observed by a number of people:

- your class teacher;
- your mentor;
- your course tutor;
- subject specialists or head teachers in the school;
- external and internal examiners;
- HMIE inspectors.

These observations, and the feedback and target-setting they give rise to, are your chance to address Element 2.4.3 and show that you can act on advice and be open to coaching and mentoring.

Observation by your class teacher

Most day-to-day observation will be done in an informal way, simply because the teacher is in the classroom with you. Unless you ask otherwise, he or she may give you only a few words of feedback. This sort of observation is valuable as the teacher will build up a comprehensive picture of your performance across the whole range of subjects and in a variety of settings – the class, the hall, the ICT suite, etc. These observations, however informal, will inevitably contribute to your assessment because the mentor is likely to discuss them with the class teacher.

You can focus these observations so that they work for you. Ask your teacher to observe you in specific sessions where you are addressing one of your targets, whether it is to teach in the ICT suite, to manage children positively in the outdoor classroom or to use a more varied range of questions. You will need to discuss your plan and give a copy of it to the teacher as part of the observation. When giving you feedback your teacher will pick out what you did well and suggest things you can do to continue progress. He or she will certainly see that you are focusing on improvement and looking for advice and this, in itself, is good practice. It would be unrealistic to expect full, detailed feedback for every lesson or session you teach and you should not assume that a lack of comment from your teacher indicates something negative. If you would like your teacher's insights about some aspect of your teaching and you have not asked him or her to observe the session, make sure you ask specific questions. Questions like 'What did you think about the worksheet I used?' or 'Do you think the tasks were at the right level for blue group?' are much more likely to have useful answers than general questions like 'How did it go?'

MINI CASE MINI CASE **MINI CASE MINI CASE** MINI CASE MINI CASE **MINI CASE**

Actually teaching in front of my teacher on first placement was agony to start with. I just hadn't expected it, really. The worst bit was that I was desperate for feedback. No – for praise. I only wanted to hear good stuff. If my teacher didn't say 'That was good' I felt despondent and I hung around hopefully at the end of every lesson. After the first week I got used to it and could discuss lessons rationally and even accept tips for the future, which was her way of giving advice. In my second week my teacher gave a sort of wave and nipped out of one lesson. I think it was the first time I realised that she wasn't scrutinising my every movement. It also made me realise I was in charge – at least for a bit.

Harbahavan, PGDE Primary

MINI CASE MINI CASE **MINI CASE MINI CASE** MINI CASE MINI CASE **MINI CASE**

In my first class I was totally relaxed about teaching in front of my class teacher because I'd worked in her class for a while. She offered reassuring comments whenever I taught. I wasn't really prepared for how different it would be when I went to another class on placement. Initially, I felt nervous teaching in front of someone else but I got used to it quickly. It was harder to get used to the way he often didn't comment about my teaching every time I taught a lesson. I found myself asking 'How was it?' all the time. As the placement went on, I realised that my teacher did comment, but just not about everything I taught and I relaxed about it. I also found that he was really pleased to be asked to observe a lesson and talk through the good and bad points after – he just liked to be asked to do it. I think he really didn't want to be over-critical and make me feel I was being observed in every lesson. The placement went really well and I learned a lot from that teacher.

Maureen, BEd

Observation by your mentor

Your mentor, or sometimes your class teacher, will do more formal observations. The number of these will vary from placement to placement. You will agree times for these in advance and make sure a copy of your planning for the session or lesson is available to your mentor at the start of the observation. These observations will usually be recorded on a sheet with a specific format (although these vary from course to course) and comments will be linked to the standards and your targets. You will be given a copy of the feedback shortly after the observation and have a chance to discuss the observation with your mentor in your mentor meeting, if not before.

Some of these observations will be general, in the sense that they are observations of you teaching a particular subject, such as PSHE, or in a particular setting, such as the outdoor classroom. The mentor will pick out particular points, usually relevant to your planning and teaching of the lessons, and link these to the standards. As a result of each observation you will be clear about some things you have done well and, probably, have a target for you to work towards.

Other observations will be focused on your particular targets, either those identified before the placement or those identified at a mentor meeting. You may want a number of observations to address a particular target, such as giving appropriate praise, or using your voice effectively, or maintaining the pace of a lesson. These observations will be particularly good for helping you to be aware of progress towards a particular standard.

Observation by your course tutor

If your ITE provider has course tutors who visit on placement, they will usually observe you teaching. This will be the same sort of formal, written observation as your mentor makes and you will be given the notes and verbal feedback after the observation. The tutor will arrange a visit in advance and may ask to see a specific part of your teaching – a particular subject, or teaching in the outdoor classroom. The tutor will want to meet your mentor and class teacher and this might influence the timing of the visit. Tutors will usually arrive slightly earlier than the observation and try to put you at your ease by chatting informally for a few minutes. You should prepare very carefully for tutor observations. Have a copy of the lesson plan available for the tutor and make sure your placement file and training plan file are available if the tutor wants them. If you are in a primary class you should probably identify a place for the tutor to sit, so that he or she does not get in the way of the lesson. These details present you as a well organised professional even before your lesson is observed.

The course tutor may well do a joint observation with your mentor, class teacher or head teacher. This means they will both observe you at the same time, with the tutor and mentor making observation notes. Both observers will then discuss the observation between themselves before giving you feedback, including the written notes. The point of an observation like this is to ensure that both the mentor and the course tutor have the same expectations about your performance and that both make the same judgements about your teaching. This is a form of moderation and helps to ensure that all trainees are judged fairly.

> MINI CASE MINI CASE MINI CASE **MINI CASE** MINI CASE MINI CASE **MINI CASE**
>
> *Tutor observations are nerve-wracking because you don't really know the tutor that well. I was always secretly slightly concerned in case I was different from all the other trainees and just didn't know it!*
>
> Ben, PGDE

> MINI CASE MINI CASE MINI CASE **MINI CASE** MINI CASE MINI CASE **MINI CASE**
>
> *My tutors were really helpful. They always gave feedback on my plans as well as the sessions. Most of the sessions where I have been observed went really well but one; when I did a Chinese New Year activity with a P1 group, it was a bit of a management disaster. I hadn't really considered that all the glittery things and gold paint would be so exciting for the children. They got a bit giddy and I didn't calm them down. I felt stressed and nervous and panicked a bit and the whole activity was disorganised, with overexcited children and me totally failing to use my key vocabulary or address my teaching objectives. I thought the tutor would be really cross and that I'd totally humiliated myself. Actually, she was fine. She did agree with my evaluation of the lesson (and it was painful to see that in writing) but she was very constructive. We identified a list of things to do to reduce my nervousness and to ensure I managed groups better. Most importantly, my tutor pointed out that not every lesson is going to go well and that sometimes, a disaster might just be the session that is observed. It didn't affect my assessment because other lessons observed were good and the tutor could see from the lesson observation sheets in my file that my mentor had observed good sessions.*
>
> Gina, Early Years PGDE (part-time)

Observation by your subject specialist or head teacher

These sessions will be formal written observations like those with your mentor. It is very useful to have a particular subject co-ordinator or phase co-ordinator look at their area of interest, especially if it is one of your target areas. Their expertise in the subject and also of observing other teachers' lessons will mean they can give you good feedback and new ideas. Prepare for these observations as you would for a mentor observation and make sure your plan is available to the observer.

Observation by your external or internal examiners

All training programmes have examiners of some sort. Internal examiners or moderators may be partnership staff or local head teachers who observe a number of trainees for moderation purposes. They will be observing to check that the expectations and judgements made by mentors and course tutors are consistent for all the trainees.

External examiners will be senior staff from other training institutions. They perform a similar moderation role on most courses. They observe to ensure that the standards for ITE are being met and that the grades awarded to trainees are consistent, not only across the course but for trainees in other programmes. Although you might not welcome a visit from an examiner you should not worry. They are very experienced and their visits protect the standard of your award by ensuring that grades are fair.

There are a number of reasons why you might have visits from examiners. The most likely reason for a visit is that you have been chosen more or less at random as part of a sample of the cohort. However, if you have experienced severe difficulties and may not achieve the Standards for ITE, then you may also have a visit from the external examiner to collect evidence to inform an examination board. This evidence will be an important part of making the decision about whether you have met the Standards for ITE.

Any visit by an external or internal examiner or moderator will be arranged in advance. They will expect to observe you teaching, talk to you, talk to your mentor or class teacher and look through your placement file and training plan. Make sure these are readily available and that you have a copy of your lesson plan ready to give your visitor. The examiner may give you feedback but you should not automatically expect detailed feedback if the main purpose of the visit is moderation.

Observation by HMIE inspectors

You may be observed by HMIE inspectors for two reasons. All ITE provision undergoes HMIE inspection and so it is possible that you will be observed as part of the inspection of your ITE provider. In this case, you will be notified in advance and the partnership will tell you very clearly what to expect and what you should prepare. The inspector may want to observe you teaching, interview you and the mentor and take a detailed look at your files. Alternatively, the inspector might ask to observe another aspect of training, such as one of your mentor meetings. If you are notified of an HMIE visit, contact your ITE provider, who will be able to tell you exactly what to expect, how long it will take and who will be involved. Your role is to ensure you are well prepared so that you are organised, professional and confident on the day. It would be unusual for inspectors to give detailed or written feedback after a visit to a trainee but they will usually give some, limited, verbal comments.

You might also be observed as part of the school's HMIE inspection. As schools receive short notice of an inspection, your placement could well fall in an inspection week. In this case the school will usually advise you about what they would like you to do that week. It is a good time to fit in and work together with the staff. Be prepared to support your teacher in any lessons that are observed or to be observed teaching yourself. Your teaching might well be confined to groups during inspection week if your teacher prefers that. Be well prepared for whatever you teach and ensure your files are available. The inspector may want to talk to you about your experience in the school. Remember that while you are not going to be the school's first priority during inspection week, HMIE will be looking at the provision made for trainees by the school. HMIE inspectors will always talk to you if they observe you teaching, but you should not expect written feedback or much detail. Having an HMIE inspection during your placement is a useful experience. You see the school at its best (well prepared) and its worst (nervous teachers). Being part of a school's HMIE inspection teaches you that inspection is a routine part of school life – and experience of an HMIE inspection is a great thing to talk about at job interviews.

Target-setting for your training

Throughout your training (and afterwards in your probation year) you will be expected to set clear targets to help you improve your performance towards all aspects of the Standards for provisional registration (and, later, full registration). Target-setting alone will not bring about improvement – it needs to lead to action. This section will help you to set realistic and demanding targets and to think through how your targets can be achieved through effective action.

Reviewing

In order to set your targets for a placement you will need to review and analyse your current performance. Before your first school placement, your mentor or tutors will help you to set appropriate targets based on some general expectations of a first placement but taking into account your previous experience.

If you are setting targets for a second, third or fourth placement, you will start by reviewing the outcomes of previous placements. With your course tutor, you will discuss your tutor's placement report from the previous placement, your observation notes, and your placement file and your own self-evaluation to identify your progress and needs. This is not to say that the beginning and end of placements are the only times to review your progress but these are times when you are particularly concerned to set targets.

Progress with the Standards

An essential part of your programme is to achieve all the Standards that lead to provisional registration. Therefore, during and after each school placement, it will be necessary for you to consider your progress against the particular Standards related to that work (refer to the *Professional Standards for Initial Teacher Education*). Mentors and course tutors will discuss school placements with you.

When considering Standards you should:

(a) know which Standards you aimed to address during this placement;
(b) look at written feedback related to the Standards, e.g. placement reports, mentor meeting notes, observations;
(c) note oral feedback from mentors and tutors.

There will be some Standards you have not had the opportunity to address (perhaps because you were not in an appropriate age phase or situation) and some that you have not succeeded in demonstrating yet. These would be good candidates for your list of targets to be identified.

Target-setting

The more precise you can be in stating what you want to achieve the easier it will be for mentors and tutors to help you and for you to measure your achievement. Get a clear picture in your mind of what success in achieving your targets will look like by being able to complete the sentence 'I will know I have achieved this target when...'

Finally, set a realistic number of targets at the beginning of the placement and expect that some others will last the duration of the placement and be more fully reviewed at the end of the placement. For instance: 'Demonstrate that they are able to use appropriate strategies to motivate and sustain the interest of all pupils during a lesson' may last all placement whereas 'Know about and understand the provision of the UN Convention on the Rights of the Child and the Children (Scotland) Act 1995' may be addressed more rapidly.

At the end of this placement, you should again review your progress and begin target-setting for your next placement.

MINI CASE MINI CASE MINI CASE **MINI CASE** MINI CASE MINI CASE **MINI CASE**

Louise had just completed her second school placement during which she had been placed with a P6 class. The placement had gone well and during her time in school she had progressed from taking parts of whole class lessons or group work to sustained periods of whole-class teaching in some curriculum areas. Although she had had to develop a range of behaviour management strategies in order to promote purposeful learning environments, her mentor reported that Louise was sensitive to the needs of her class, demonstrated and promoted positive values and set high expectations. She had developed a pleasant relationship with the children.

Louise's mentor suggested that her targets included:

- continuing to develop behaviour management strategies (Element 2.2.2);
- learning how to develop liaison between home and school (Element 1.2.2).

Louise understood that her pupils' attitudes and behaviour are influenced as much by their everyday lives outside school as by the time spent in school. Encouragement, support and guidance from both home and school are crucial and can have a significant impact on their learning. Louise appreciated the need for establishing a purposeful learning environment and that she needed a greater range of strategies in order to ensure that her pupils were always interested, motivated and remained on task. This would help them to learn effectively, not disrupt others and make significant progress.

Louise has read of the importance attached to teachers finding ways to communicate with parents and carers, especially those unwilling or unable to offer adequate levels of support. She also read that to achieve Element 2.2.2 she must demonstrate a range of strategies to promote good behaviour in a wide range of contexts.

In order to achieve the targets suggested, Louise began to make them more specific.

She arranged focused observations of experienced teachers in order to see how they dealt with specific aspects of behaviour management – settling children at the start of lessons, grouping children for practical activities, managing transitions between phases of the lesson, maintaining a brisk pace, using the voice effectively, using praise and encouragement, asking questions, intervening when children stray off task. She decided to talk through the school's behaviour policy with her mentor at the beginning of her next placement.

When dealing with parents, Louise decided to become pro-active and talk informally with parents collecting their children from school. She decided to ask if she could write trial reports on some pupils and compare her efforts with those of her class teacher. She determined to talk to her mentor about how the school dealt with problems that necessitated formal discussions with parents. She looked forward to attending her first parents' evening.

Finally, at the end of your course, following your final placement in school, you must meet target-setting requirements for completion of your Profile. This asks you to set targets for your probationary year. These can be:

- areas of the standards where you have had little experience (such as a particular foundation subject you have not taught) work in the outdoor classroom or developing your expertise in working with parents;
- areas of the standards you found challenging throughout your ITE and want to strengthen, such as behaviour management or the way you use your voice;
- areas of interest to you, such as your specialist subject or special needs.

Mentor meetings, professional relationships and advice

Some of the most important times in your training are your mentor meetings. These review progress, refocus your targets and maintain your progress towards achieving the standards. It is very important that you agree a convenient, regular time and place for these at the start of your placement. You will also want to keep a record of your mentor meetings as evidence of your professional development, the actions you have taken to meet targets and progress in setting new targets. Some courses provide a special form for this (see Figure 6.1 below), but you can use plain paper. Agree with your mentor who will take the notes and check you agree about what is recorded before you conclude the meeting.

Log of BEd/PGDE Trainee–Mentor Meeting
This record should be maintained by the trainee and signed by both participants. The top copy should go in the placement file, the pink copy in the mentor's training file and the blue copy should be retained for the course tutor.

Date: 20 June 2005	Trainee: Belinda Noyes, PGDE Mentor: June Smith	St Joseph's Primary School

Focus for discussion:

The science observation done this week
IEPs
School-based tasks

Summary of discussion:

The science observation identified differentiation for the most and least able as something to work on but showed progress in organising resources and managing the children.

We talked about the upcoming Book Week and what costume I might try.

We discussed the children in my class who have IEPs and how I can incorporate some of the main points from the IEPs in my lesson plans.

One of my school tasks is to examine some IEPs.

Action points (referenced to the standards):

Meet Mrs James (Special Needs Co-ordinator) to look at IEP writer and review some of my lesson plans.
June to organise ((1.1.2, 2.1.4).

June will observe my literacy next week, looking at the differentiation (2.1.1).

I will be taking the fairy tales activity on Wednesday and the horror activity on Friday in Book Week. These activities which demonstrate my teaching work (2.1.3).

Signed (Mentor) .... Signed (Trainee) ....

Figure 6.1. Sample mentor meeting notes

When you begin a placement you will have a set of expectations for that placement. It is important to ensure that you keep these, and your personal targets, in mind. One way to do this is to work out a rough timetable of mentor agenda items. You will not use them all but it means that you will not get to the end of the placement and suddenly find that you have three days left to do all your school-based tasks, look at the school citizenship policy and teach RE.

On her second placement of five weeks Belinda's planned agendas looked like this (see Figure 6.2):

Week	Routine items	Things I want to focus on if other issues do not arise
1	The requirements for the placement. My personal placement targets. School welcome pack. What I will observe this week, and my first teaching experiences.	The behaviour policy. School SEN policy.
2	My observations so far of core subjects. Plan to get school tasks (pupil profiles) done.	My teaching of group guided reading and the mathematics mental/oral.
3	No meeting.	
4	Observations of my teaching in the last fortnight. Progress on school tasks.	IEPs and meeting with the SENCO.
5	Observations of me teaching this week. Concluding school tasks.	My placement report.

Figure 6.2. Agenda items

Assessment of your placement

Your placement will be assessed against the Standards for Initial Teacher Education. Each placement may have different requirements and not every placement will address all the Standards, so it is important you are aware of which Standards will be assessed during your placement. Completing specific school tasks will also be a requirement of the placement.

For a shorter placement, your mentor will usually write a report towards the end of the placement. The format of this varies from course to course, but you will usually be assessed against each section of the Standards for ITE and comments will be made about your progress in each area.

1. Professional attributes.
2. Professional knowledge and understanding.
3. Professional skills:
   – planning;

– teaching;
– assessing, monitoring and feedback;
– reviewing teaching;
– learning environment;
– team work.

You may be graded against each section of the standards or against each standard. The grades will usually be:

1. Satisfactory.
2. Unsatisfactory.

Each course will have a slightly different format and grading system, so be sure to review the assessment forms and criteria before the placement. Examples are provided below, but they may be slightly different from those on your training course.

If you are doing a longer placement, you may well have an interim report in the middle of the placement. This supplements the meetings you have with your mentor and ensures you review your placement in good time. If there are any areas for serious concern, you will be aware of them and can work with your mentor to address them.

These interim and final placement reports (profiles, or assessments) will form a valuable part of your training plan as they are evidence that you have addressed certain standards.

The assessment of your placement will be evidence-based. The sources of evidence will be the formal observations of your teaching made during the placement, discussion with your class teacher about what he or she has observed, records of mentor meetings and evidence you have collected in your placement file, including lesson plans, assessment records, mock reports and school tasks. If you are unsure how to demonstrate that you have achieved a standard, your course handbook probably gives more guidance about evidence for each standard.

School Experience Report (School)

STUDENT – JENNY XXX   **PGDE**   STAGE **P5**

S= Satisfactory U = Unsatisfactory

1 PROFESSIONAL KNOWLEDGE AND UNDERSTANDING

Curriculum;

Jenny has demonstrated a good understanding of the curriculum and has used curriculum documents to plan all her lessons. She has begun to match the levels to the needs of the children in the class but needs to develop further her skills in adapting materials to suit a range of needs.   **S**

Education systems and professional responsibilities;

Jenny has taken her professional responsibilities very seriously whilst at the school. She has contributed to the positive ethos in the class and has worked well with the classroom assistants and the SEN in the class.   **S**

Principles and perspectives.

Although aware of the main theories of learning, she needs to take them into consideration when planning lessons.   **S**

2 PROFESSIONAL SKILLS AND ABILITIES

Teaching and Learning;

Jenny has planned and delivered a series of lessons in language and maths. Her planning was effective and her lessons delivered competently. She needs to develop a more creative approach to maintain the interest of all the children and to break up her teaching into smaller sections to cater for the attention span of children of this age.

She is able to talk to the children in a way that makes them feel valued and uses her voice well to suit the situation. Her story telling is particularly good and she holds the children entranced with the different voices she employs.

$\boxed{\text{S}}$

Classroom organisation and management;

Poor organisation initially led to a range of problems in her lessons but following advice and observation of the teacher's strategies, she has shown some improvement. Jenny has still not been able to organise her lessons to a satisfactory level and needs to be more careful with her preparation and planning to avoid the mistakes she is making in class. Jenny found managing the behaviour in this lively class difficult. She has undertaken to use a variety of strategies in consultation with myself and the class teacher and has begun to take control more effectively but needs to maintain consistency of approach for the behaviour to improve further.

$\boxed{\text{U}}$

Using your professional placement report

When you have your professional placement report you can use it to set specific targets for your next placement, as evidence towards the completion of the Standards for ITE and to inform your completion of the Final Profile.

Problems during placement

In one sense, all placements present problems for you to solve. Education is, in itself, problematic and you, like the children, learn by setting yourself new tasks and problems. Unfortunately, sometimes difficulties can arise during placement that threaten to affect your progress. The very best way to deal with problems is to prevent them arising. This is a matter of being very clear about your targets, your expectations, your course and what your placement school has to offer. You should also know who to go to in the case of difficulties and exactly what to do if you have to be absent from school for some reason. Read your course documentation carefully before you start your placement.

Unfortunately, at some time during your placement you may feel that you have a problem or difficulty with it. If this happens to you there are a number of things you can do.

- The most common areas for difficulties with placements are allocation of placement, relationships with class teachers, tutors or mentors, assessment of your placement and behaviour management in class. There are sections in this book you may find helpful with these issues. Read the relevant section and consider your problem against this background. A little more research may help you solve your problem.
- See any problem as a test of your ability to demonstrate your professional values and practice. This does not make any problem go away, but it does get you in the right frame of mind to solve it positively, and maintain good relationships.
- Think carefully about whether you really do have a problem with your placement. If the issue annoying you is a result of, perhaps, a comparison with a friend, you might be placing undue emphasis on a minor

issue. Always consider this possibility. Teaching placement is a very pressurised experience and some people respond excessively to minor irritations.

- You may have problems during placement that are not directly caused by the placement but affect it seriously – illness, bereavement, etc. Make sure you discuss these with your mentor and make the necessary arrangements. Life happens!
- If you feel there is a problem with your placement that is affecting your training, you should talk to your mentor about it in the first instance. Do not let a problem grumble on throughout your placement without saying anything. If you do this you will have a miserable, resentful placement – probably unnecessarily.
- Your mentor really is your first port of call to discuss problems during placement. If you go straight to other members of staff or to the head teacher before consulting your mentor you could cause offence.
- When you raise a problem with your mentor, make sure you do it as a fellow professional. Make sure you do not accuse individuals, become overwrought or apportion blame. State clearly what your problem is and, if possible, suggest possible solutions or ask your mentor to help you identify possible actions. This shows you are really trying to seek a solution.
- Choose your time to raise a problem carefully. Avoid the temptation to share an important issue in passing during break or in the corridor. Instead you might arrange a brief meeting after school or wait for a mentor meeting.
- Your problem may be such that you cannot discuss it with your mentor. In this case you need to talk to your course tutor or course co-ordinator. It is very important that you read your course documentation and talk to the right person – this may be a course tutor, personal tutor or headteacher.
- If you choose to confide your problem to your class teacher make sure you are thoughtful and professional in the way you do so.
- Whoever you discuss your problem with will treat it confidentially and professionally. You must do the same within school.
- If you feel your problem is serious and you have not been able to resolve it with your mentor and course tutor you should write to your course leader and ask him or her to help you solve the problem.
- Finally, and this really is if all else has failed, your course will have a complaints procedure. You can use this if you feel you have been unfairly treated.
- Accept that schools are not perfect and be prepared to make an effort to resolve problems. Never give up because you have encountered difficulty. Look for ways to get around it.
- Never, never, never just walk out of a placement, whatever you feel. This is always unjustifiable, unprofessional behaviour.
- Congratulate yourself when you are able to resolve problems effectively. This is a real professional skill.

REFLECTIVE TASK

Identify one target for improvement in your professional skills: planning, teaching, assessing, reviewing, learning environment or team work. This target may be one of your key priorities for a first placement or a target arising from a previous placement. An example might be 'To promote positive behaviour in my P3 class'.

- Review the following issues in relation to *your* target.
- What is already in place in your setting? (Behaviour policy, observe the teacher to see what *he* does.)
- What you know about frameworks for classroom discipline. (www.behaviour4learning.ac.uk)
- What opportunities you have identified to work on in this target. (First whole class session, group support work.)
- What feedback you can get about your target. (Will your teacher or mentor observe?)

A SUMMARY OF **KEY POINTS**

> Each trainee's training is different because each trainee is different. Placements are chosen to meet your training needs.

> As you go through your ITE you will compile a training plan (or record of professional development). This will include your achievements and targets. Your targets will help you to address the standards for ITE.

> To make the most of your professional placement you must be sure you know what the requirements of the placement are and what your targets are. You can then plan to achieve them.

> Your mentor is an important person in your training. He or she will help you to set and monitor targets and arrange placement experiences. Your mentor will be involved in your assessment. Mentor meetings are a key training experience and to use them well you should be prepared and keep records of meetings and agreed targets.

> You will be observed teaching on placement by a number of people. Make sure you know why you are being observed and prepare well for your observation.

> Your mentor, class teacher and course tutor may be involved in your assessment. Make sure they have evidence of your achievements and can easily look at your training plan and placement file.

> Your placement assessment is an important document and you will use it as evidence towards the standards and to set targets for future teaching and professional development.

> Professional problems can be sorted out in a professional way. Deal with any problems swiftly and positively so that you can move on and get the most from your placement.

Resources

The General Teaching Council (Scotland) – GTCS – is a good site for information about standards and general teaching issues – http://www.gtcs.org.uk/About_GTCS/About_GTCS.asp

The Learning and Teaching Scotland website has plenty of advice and information about assessment – and links to other government sites – www.ltscotland.org.uk

www.behaviour4learning is a site which provides links to relevant resources online to improve classroom behaviour.

Teacher Support Line

There is a new charity called Teacher Support Scotland that is being developed to provide independent support for teachers. Check the website at http://www.teachersupport.info/scotland.

7
The challenges of placement

As your training proceeds you will find some aspects more challenging than others. In this chapter we address some of the significant areas of professional activity on placement. By the end of this chapter you should:

- **know how to prepare for working well with other adults;**
- **know some strategies for managing children's behaviour;**
- **know what to do if you encounter a child protection issue.**

Working with other adults

Some of the benchmark standards for Initial Teacher Education deal with working with other adults.

Education systems and professional responsibilities – 1.2.2
- Demonstrate an awareness of their responsibilities for contributing to the ethos of the school for example by promoting positive relationships between staff, pupils and parents.
- Demonstrate an understanding of the roles and responsibilities of staff within school including their responsibility for school improvement.
- Know about the roles of other professionals and how to work with them.

Teaching and Learning – 2.1.5;
- Demonstrate that they are able to work co-operatively in the classroom and in multi-agency settings with other professionals, staff and parents.

Organisation and Management – 2.2.1
- Know how to co-operate in planning and organising working arrangements involving as appropriate, nursery nurses, classroom assistants, parent helpers and other ancillary staff.

On placement you will be working with a range of other adults. They may include adults who do not teach but are extremely valuable members of staff:

- school secretaries or administrators;
- lunchtime supervisors;
- school caretakers;
- before or after school carers or club managers;
- non-teacher coaching or teaching staff.

You need to find out about the roles of these members of staff and how they affect you. It is important that you establish a similar relationship with them as you have with your teacher, so you need to know details. For instance, how does the school administrator manage the lunch money? How are registers sent to the secretary? How should you manage the transition to lunchtime/after school activities? How do you manage the transition to netball coaching time? What do you have to do to ensure these practices are maintained?

Another category of adults will work with you in the classroom or setting. These will include:

- Early Years practitioners;
- classroom assistants;
- school teaching staff such as the SENCO, teachers from other parts of the school such as a behaviour, communication or learning unit, a special needs teaching assistant;
- visiting professionals such as psychologists, support teachers, social workers, etc.;
- parents.

Early Years practitioners

If you are undertaking a placement in an Early Years setting such as a Nursery class, nursery nurses, practitioners, assistants or facilitators will be part of your placement. They will be part of the teaching team and you will usually do your planning together as a team. At first it may be difficult to identify the differences between the roles of the teacher and other practitioners. All will set up resources, plan activities, make assessment notes and take time out to observe children. All will manage behaviour, deal with incidents and talk to parents. However, the teacher will lead the planning and assessment and manage the overall situation. This is the role you are aiming for, so you too must learn to work well in a team. Practitioners may work as a full time member of the teaching team or in one of the ways described below.

Classroom assistants

Classroom assistants have a vital role to play throughout the primary school and there are now more of them in the profession than ever before. Classroom assistants do not receive training prior to taking up the post although they may be required to complete some training once in post. They will be deployed strategically to meet the needs of the school or particular pupils.

- Classroom assistants may spend all or most of their time working with a specific class or specific classes or groups of children. This is a regular arrangement that allows you to plan for classroom assistant involvement.
- They may be given a range of tasks e.g. preparing materials or resources for the teacher; putting up displays; working with a group of pupils or an individual child on a task set by and monitored by the teacher. They may for example work with individual children entering data onto a computer as part of a science lesson or work with a group of children on a practical maths task. The presence of an 'extra pair of hands' can be invaluable in lessons involving practical activities.
- They may have other areas of responsibility such as playground supervision or lunch time duties and so may have to leave the class at specific times to allow them to have their breaktime.
- Classroom assistants may be given a regular role within the class or school e.g. supervising the lending of library books, collecting children from various classes for music lessons.
- Some classroom assistants are employed specifically to help a child with additional support needs and will remain with that child all the time. They may help the child with practical issues such as movement from a wheelchair to a desk, assist with toilet needs and medication, and will be available to help that child with work in class. They may work with other children in the class in small groups but the needs of their specific charge must always come first. If they attend the child during breaktime and lunchtime, they will be out of class at a different time to have their own breaks.
- Classroom assistants may make and prepare resources for teachers but may not expect to do the same for student teachers. If help is offered, make sure your requests are reasonable and made in good time –

do not expect instant miracles or make impossible demands.

- In infant classes, there may be trained nursery assistants working with the class for all or part of the week. You may be expected to plan work for them but check with your teacher as they might have dedicated tasks already.
- Children attending special units for part of the week may receive assistance from the unit in the classroom as well. In this case you will need to work with them in your planning to ensure continuity and understanding.

As part of your induction you need to find out which classroom assistants work in your class and what their role is. You should do this by asking the teacher first of all, and it would also be useful to ask the teaching assistants to explain their role to you. You should ask:

- What classroom assistants or Early Years practitioners work in this class or setting?
- What is the role of each practitioner or classroom assistant?
- If the classroom assistant's role is with a particular child or children, how does this affect others they work with?
- Does the classroom assistant have special responsibility for ASL or EAL?
- When does each practitioner or classroom assistant work with this class or pupil?
- What role does the classroom assistant or practitioner take in planning and assessment?
- What role does the classroom assistant or practitioner take in different parts of the sessions? Do practitioners or classroom assistants support individuals during the mental/oral and plenaries, work with groups or take groups of children out of the classroom?
- What will the classroom assistant/practitioner prepare? Some classroom assistants prepare all the activities for their intervention programme but most will expect to participate in putting out resources for some activities.

As you build up responsibility for planning sessions and sequences of lessons you will be working closely with other adults. In an Early Years setting this may mean agreeing to the outline planning for each activity and session but some of the detail will be planned by other practitioners. You will need to see this planning so that you know what is happening in the setting, as your teacher would do. In a primary class you will be planning for classroom assistants. When you are planning for someone else it is vital that you are very clear about what role you want them to play and what you want the children to learn – this is a basic professional role but it is not as simple as it sounds in a busy class. You cannot expect classroom assistants to read your mind and a very common mistake is to make assumptions about what a classroom assistant knows and fail to explain properly what is required. This puts the classroom assistant or practitioner in a difficult position and they may not be able to do what you want.

We recommend you use a planning format such as the one given in Chapter 3 to make sure that the learning objectives (or outcomes) of a lesson are clear, that the classroom assistant knows exactly what language to use, what support to offer. Your classroom assistant may not be used to having a written plan for lessons but you want to make quite sure you are explicit and a planning sheet is one way to do this. Using a sheet like this is useful for all these reasons but it also has a training role for you. If you become used to planning in detail for a classroom assistant early in your career, you are more likely to continue to think through these issues, even when you do not use a planning sheet for classroom assistants.

You will find that many Early Years practitioners and classroom assistants you work with are well qualified and very experienced. This can feel intimidating when you are starting your placement. However, experienced classroom assistants or practitioners are a real asset. You will benefit from working alongside them and learning from their expertise. You are training for a slightly different role, as teacher, and you are not competing with classroom assistants or practitioners. When working with classroom assistants or practitioners you have a responsibility to be professional, well organised and to behave confidently because to do otherwise undermines their work as well as your own.

MINI CASE MINI CASE MINI CASE **MINI CASE** MINI CASE MINI CASE **MINI CASE**

On my first placement in the Nursery unit everyone worked together. Each practitioner planned for one area of learning each week and managed a teacher-directed and a couple of child-led activities each session. We sort of discussed them at the Thursday meeting then planned our own. At first I thought everyone did exactly the same but after a couple of meetings I realised that Jill (the teacher) steered the planning and used the documents and records to plan. She was really leading the planning and also looking at everyone's plans on a Friday. I worked up to it and did it with her.

Sara, PGDE

MINI CASE MINI CASE MINI CASE **MINI CASE** MINI CASE MINI CASE **MINI CASE**

I was a classroom assistant myself before this course so it has been strange doing the PGDE. In my second placement I had a full-time classroom assistant (Bev) in the P1 class. Actually I found planning for her a bit of a burden. I mean it was great having her. I did things I couldn't have done on my own and I know it improved the children's learning but there were days when I felt that planning for her was just the last straw. My own experience as a classroom assistant helped me to be clear about exactly what I wanted Bev to do and to make sure I talked with her before and after lessons. Even that, though, was something I had to practise. I found Bev very reassuring. She was positive and calm but when I was a classroom assistant myself, I never realised that working with a classroom assistant would be an effort.

Molly, PGDE

MINI CASE MINI CASE MINI CASE **MINI CASE** MINI CASE MINI CASE **MINI CASE**MINI CASE

In my school there are 12 classroom assistants. Some are assigned to particular classes and some to particular children. Two of them are specially trained to do the intervention programmes for struggling children and work with groups outside the class. I worked with two of the classroom assistants, one (Ellie) in class supporting a child with autistic spectrum disorder and one (Nerika) who did guided reading. I planned for Ellie in all my lesson plans as a differentiation issue and so I asked her to look at my daily plans. She supported her child but also the whole group and it was important that they didn't depend on her too much and addressed the objectives themselves. With Nerika, I had to monitor the guided reading and get feedback from her. I found it quite difficult to suggest texts as she knew them better than me. I became confident working with Ellie and Nerika when I convinced myself that I had nothing to prove. Both classroom assistants were very supportive to me.

Jo, PGDE

School teaching staff

Staff working alongside you in your class may include EAL teachers, the ASL co-ordinator and teachers from specialist units (such as behaviour support). You need to discuss their roles in much the same way as you would the classroom assistant's role. Make sure you know what they aim to do, which children they are targeting and how they work with you. This may mean that they observe and assess certain children, that they support children in doing activities you are teaching or that they plan, in cooperation with you, for slightly different activities for the target children. Specialist teachers may also come into your class to advise you and help you differentiate for certain children.

Visiting professionals

Educational psychologists, curriculum support advisers and social workers may come to your class for a variety of reasons. Their visits may be part of a school policy implementation or there may be concern about particular children. You should discuss the role of each professional with your teacher and, where possible, shadow him/her at meetings in which they are involved. However, some meetings (for instance those about child protection issues) may be confidential and so sensitive that it would not be appropriate for you to attend. In this case you can still discuss the processes for this sort of meeting without discussing the content. Ensure you know the role of each visiting professional you encounter, how their involvement was triggered, how long they have been involved with the class or child and what the likely actions resulting from such involvement will be.

Parents

Parents may also work in your classroom voluntarily. They will not have had experience a classroom assistant has had, so it is doubly important to ensure you know their accustomed role and that you are very clear about what you would like them to do. In some cases parents come in to work on a particular school initiative, such as a story sack project in the Early Years or a talking book project with infants. Find out about these initiatives. In other cases parents come in to assist with a certain lesson. For instance, a parent might come in on one morning a week to play the guitar for the class music session or to supervise handwriting with groups of children. Having parents in classes carries certain child protection and confidentiality issues and all parents coming into class will complete a criminal record disclosure process and have a discussion with a member of school staff about maintaining confidentiality.

Management of children's behaviour

Managing the behaviour of the children in your class is a key issue. You need to demonstrate certain benchmarks related to this –

Professional Knowledge and Understanding –
Curriculum – 1.1.2

- Know how to promote and support the individual development, well-being and social competence of all the pupils in their class and show commitment to raising these pupil's expectations of themselves and others.

Professional Skills and Attributes –
Teaching and Learning- 2.1.4

- Set expectations and a pace of work which makes appropriate demands on all pupils.

Classroom Organisation and Management – 2.2.2

- Manage pupils behaviour fairly, sensitively and consistently by the use of appropriate rewards and sanctions and know when it is necessary to seek advice.

Professional Values and Personal Commitment – 3.1

- Value and demonstrate a commitment to social justice, inclusion and protecting and caring for children.

The school behaviour policy

The first document of interest to you in a new placement is the school behaviour policy. This sets out the school's aims in terms of the ethos and behaviour of the school and the sort of relationships the staff want to establish. It also sets out the strategies that are used, consistently and by all teachers, to establish and maintain a positive ethos and good relationships. Read this document as soon as possible and observe how your teacher implements the rewards and sanctions described in the policy.

Establishing expectations – the class teacher contract

You will undertake your placement in a class or setting run by a successful teacher. The class will be well behaved and working successfully but each class will be slightly different. For a start, each teacher establishes different expectations of the children at the start of the year and enforces these. This is how the children recognise what is acceptable and learn exactly what is not acceptable. Some teachers will explicitly negotiate rules for acceptable behaviour at the beginning of the year, display these on the wall and review them periodically. This is useful because it gives the teacher a chance to discuss rules positively and make clear the point of each rule, such as 'Talk quietly so that others can be heard' rather than 'No shouting'. However, all teachers have an unspoken contract with their class that ensures that the children behave well as long as they are engaged and interested. If either the teacher or children fail to deliver their part of the contract, the balance of good behaviour may break down.

PRACTICAL TASK PRACTICAL TASK PRACTICAL TASK PRACTICAL TASK PRACTICAL TASK

Observe your class to ensure you know the terms of the unwritten contract between teacher and children – the expectations, rules and sanctions used on a daily basis. Use the questions below as guidance.

- What are the rules for talking in a session/lesson?
- How do children know when to pay attention to the teacher talking?
- How does the teacher know when children are bored or not understanding work?
- What are the rules about taking turns in talking during a group or class meeting?
- What are the rules for moving around the class?
- What are the rules for going out of the class during a session/lesson?
- What are the rules for moving equipment around?

Watch the teacher teaching and try to work out the scale of sanctions and rewards in the class. How does the teacher reward good attention or performance? Identify the rewards your teacher uses that you will need to add to the list. Rewards might be:

- making eye contact with the child;
- making eye contact and smiling;
- making eye contact and nodding or other gestures;
- using verbal rewards (praise) – 'Well done', 'Good', 'Spot on', 'Lovely', etc.;
- using small physical gestures such as patting an arm when praising;
- giving a token reward – a house point or sticker (these may add up to a larger reward in a school system);
- drawing the rest of the class or group's attention to good behaviour or work – 'Look at Ben's great picture!';
- putting a reward sticker or points on to a class chart;
- earning 'golden time' or some other privilege;
- sending the child to some higher authority to show good work (such as the deputy head);
- mentioning or rewarding good behaviour in a key stage or class assembly.

Each time the teacher uses one of these rewards, as he or she does hundreds of times a day, it ensures that the behaviour that was praised or rewarded is more likely to occur again.

- What does the teacher do when a child does not meet the expectations of the teacher in terms of behaviour? Here are some sanctions:
- making eye contact with the child;
- making eye contact and frowning;
- making eye contact and nodding or other gestures;
- using the name of a child who is misbehaving to get their attention;
- using verbal sanctions – 'Please don't...', 'Not now', etc.;
- not giving a token reward – a house point or sticker;
- giving a token punishment such as writing the child's name on the board (there will usually be a system of how many names are acceptable in a day);
- spending a minute or so away from activities (time out);
- drawing the rest of the class or group's attention to poor behaviour or work – 'What should Ben do?';
- taking a child aside for a quiet word about unacceptable behaviour;
- keeping a child in class during playtime;
- sending the child to some higher authority to prevent disruption (such as the deputy head – but never send a child out of the class unaccompanied);
- calling another teacher to come and fetch a child.

When you observe your teacher, take about 20 minutes to keep a tally of how many rewards are given out (tiny little things like a word or a gesture) and how many sanctions are used. You will invariably find that many more rewards are used than sanctions. This is called 'catching them being good'. If you find yourself beginning to nag at children, continually criticise or keep repeating the same names you need to check whether you are being very negative. This will not change behaviour. Start to scan the class routinely every minute or so and catch someone being good. The reward of a smile, a nod or a well chosen word does more to establish good behaviour than nagging.

The list of rules, rewards and sanctions you compile is essential knowledge in any class if you are to step into the teacher's shoes.

Acting like a teacher – your part of the contract

As a trainee you want the children to see you as the teacher and respect you as a teacher. Children are certainly not afraid of their teachers so why do they respect and behave well for them? Firstly, because teachers act like teachers, sending out all sorts of subtle signals that indicate they know what they are doing, have authority and expect children to behave well. You need to send out these signals if you want the children to recognise your authority. Here are some strategies for acting like the teacher in a class or Early Years setting.

- Know the children by name. If you know names you have a good start. 'Please sit down, Jamie' is so much more authoritative than 'Please sit down, no, not you, *you*'. If necessary label children with stickers with their names on. Thank and praise children by name, too.
- Look like a teacher – this does not mean a new wardrobe, just sensible choices that show you recognise the dress code in the school and fit into the teacher category of adults.
- Move confidently and avoid skulking in the background. If you are feeling nervous, stand up so the children can see you, rather than sitting down.
- Use your voice confidently. Your voice is your best tool and needs to vary in pace, tone, pitch and volume. The children respond to changes in your voice, not shouting. So sometimes dropping your voice to a whisper attracts attention better than shouting.
- Make sure you have a signal for getting the attention of the whole class. If your teacher uses clapping, hands in the air or a tambourine, you should start by using that signal even if it is not really your style. Everyone develops their own attention-grabbing signal eventually. Some teachers say 'OK, right!', 'Children!', 'Listen, please'; some snap their fingers, clap and sing to get attention. You may not find out what your personal signal is until you hear the children imitating you. All are effective when used confidently.
- Do not begin to talk to the class or group until they are silent. Wait, even if it seems to take ages. If you talk while the children are talking it signals that it is acceptable to ignore you and that you are not a real teacher.
- Know the systems in the class or setting. If you do not know something make sure you ask the children to tell you in a confident manner. 'Jennie, please put this buggy away where it belongs' is confident. 'I'm not sure where these go – do you know?' is not.
- Use eye contact, without staring, as a way to engage, interest and bring children back on task.
- Have a range of facial expression, ranging from a relaxed, open smile to a frown or shocked look.
- Follow the children's established routine and make it clear you know what happens and what you expect.
- Maintain the same expectations about behaviour as the teacher (you will have observed these very carefully).
- Clearly state the behaviour you expect at the start of each activity. Relate this to class rules where possible.
- Scan the class so that you can spot (and reward) good behaviour and keep an eye out for those misbehaving or children who are off task. Developing this scanning involves looking up and around at regular intervals. It is known as teacher radar.
- Act purposefully. Know what you are doing and get on with it. Going straight into what you have planned engages interest and prevents disruption.
- Prepare interesting, relevant lessons that everyone can participate in. This is, of course, the big challenge

but it is the child who is bored, left out, struggling or clueless who shows inappropriate behaviour – and becomes your nightmare.

- Be prepared for the unexpected. If you are ever in a situation where you do not know what to do, then do something purposeful – a few action rhymes, a bit of times tables practice, a team quiz or reading some poems can fill most gaps without undermining your authority. You should always have some emergency filler like this ready.

These sorts of strategies make your authority and your role as the teacher clear. However, you must also be aware of the ways in which you can step out of role and lose control. Do **not**, therefore:

- plan work they cannot do, do not understand or find boring;
- fail to explain what you want and they should do, so that they are confused;
- waste their time by not getting down to things at once;
- try to use inducements or rewards in an attempt to be liked;
- beg feebly, rather than telling: 'Will you...?' can be answered with 'No!'. 'Please...' cannot;
- enter into arguments with children. You know best because you are the teacher – never argue with a child;
- overpraise everything so that your praise has no meaning;
- ignore or not recognise bad behaviour that should be dealt with;
- use sarcasm or irony that the children cannot understand or make jokes at their expense;
- act inconsistently or unfairly;
- fail to distinguish yourself – children need to engage with your character through your voice and gestures: this is often what makes lessons interesting.

MINI CASE MINI CASE MINI CASE **MINI CASE** MINI CASE MINI CASE **MINI CASE**

In my first placement I was nervous. I really didn't want to seem like a know-all in front of my teacher or other students. I made the classic mistake of being too equivocal and not establishing myself as a teacher. I asked them to do things then didn't follow up if they ignored me and I couldn't get them all quiet at once. The children sussed my nerves at once and were really rowdy. I couldn't understand it at all. They were angels for Jean (the teacher) and devils for me. After a week or so Jean and my mentor sat me down and talked it through. We came up with a plan. My first aim was to get them quiet and set a simple task. I would not talk over them but I would really act, so that my voice was much more colourful. It was terrifying the first time. I had to name some naughty ones and get Jean to sit with them but I did it. I worked on using my voice, radiating authority and getting them quiet all placement. It was my hardest and most important lesson but I can honestly say it has not been an issue since.

Niki, BEd.

MINI CASE MINI CASE MINI CASE **MINI CASE** MINI CASE MINI CASE **MINI CASE**

I was told on my course 'Don't smile until Christmas', a humorous way of saying that you need to establish your authority before you can have a warm relationship. But it didn't stop me getting it wrong. I was too friendly and let the children in the nursery treat me differently to the other staff. They would put their hands in my pockets and do other little things that I now see were inappropriate. After a week or so I could see that I simply wasn't getting their attention like the other staff. They would ignore me and I didn't know what to do. I talked to Amy (my mentor) who helped me sort it out. It was much harder than starting out well and I struggled with establishing my authority for the whole five weeks. I didn't make the same mistake the next time.

Billie, PGDE

MINI CASE MINI CASE MINI CASE **MINI CASE** MINI CASE MINI CASE **MINI CASE**

I am a lively person in real life but in class my voice just seemed to shut down. I couldn't seem to keep attention or command the children. My voice was described by a colleague I knew well as 'wimpy'. I was devastated. I did some voice training at the university and on my final placement I just went for it. I acted the whole placement, varying my voice in volume and pitch. Looking back, I feel like I was amplifying my character at the children by using my voice. I suppose that is what you need to do – exaggerate expression and intonation so that all the children in a class are engaged. I still can't believe I was that wimpy. I am still a quiet teacher and keep a quiet class, but my voice and gestures are engaging and not boring.

Ulrika, Probationary teacher

MINI CASE MINI CASE MINI CASE **MINI CASE** MINI CASE MINI CASE **MINI CASE**

I consciously imitated my teacher on first placement. She did 'Heads, fingers, knees and toes' (a sort of action rhyme) to get the attention of the children. I did this too and it helped me establish myself. In my second placement I had an older class and used 'OK, listen' because it was the wording the teacher used to get attention. It worked well for me, although the first couple of times I had to wait quite a long time. Now I have my own class I just raise a hand in the air to get attention. It suits the calm sort of ethos I like in class. I think we all find our own style.

Rina, Probationary teacher

Dealing with difficult behaviour

You are not the only factor in managing children's behaviour in a classroom. For very young children in the Early Years Stage, inducting children into what behaviours are and are not acceptable is a major part of the curriculum. Even if you have planned interesting content and presented it well, there will be some children whose behaviour is unacceptable some of the time and in some classes this will represent a significant challenge. You need to learn how to deal with this gradually.

At the start of your placement you must recognise that you are not alone and seek the support of the teacher. First, you need to watch your teacher carefully to identify whose behaviour is difficult and how the teacher deals with it. Some children will have recognised difficulties with their behaviour that have resulted in their being put on the ASL register. In this case they will usually have individual education plans (IEPs) that you need to look at and accommodate in your planning. Some children will also have support from a teaching assistant and behaviour support adviser. You should talk to these people and make sure you know the strategies that they find are working.

When you have identified what the teacher's expectations are, how he or she manages behaviour in class, who finds good behaviour difficult and how the teacher deals with this, you will be starting to teach sessions or lessons. It is important that you take the teacher's role to establish your authority but you do not need to do this unsupported. Ask your teacher to be on hand and discuss what you will do in a number of situations.

If a child acts inappropriately there are a number of ways you can handle the situation.

- Ignore the inappropriate behaviour – but return to discuss it later, probably in private.
- Pass it off without undue emphasis, perhaps saying something like, 'I don't think I caught that . . .'. This gives the offender a chance to reconsider.
- Act quickly but briefly to administer a routine warning or punishment (such as a name on the board) and move swiftly on to continue what you are doing without making the incident significant.
- Assert your authority in one way or another, perhaps by looking shocked or astonished or indicating disapproval. You should only do this where you are not going to generate a conflict you cannot win and are not going to make the whole experience an interesting situation for the child.
- Separate the child from the others and deal privately with the issue so that the child is not performing for an audience.

If you are worried about a particular child or group of children in the class, make sure you are in control of the situation, have considered where they are sitting and with whom and, as you build confidence, ask your teacher to sit with those children or nearby. As your confidence develops you may still want to enlist the teacher to support you by identifying a point at which a child has had enough attention for bad behaviour and will be quietly put into the charge of the teacher. Even when your teacher is not in the class with you, when you are teaching confidently, you should always know where to find him or her (or someone standing in for them) and be able to send two children to get them.

When dealing with poor behaviour it is very important you are assertive in your manner and the way you discuss an incident of bad behaviour.

- Summarise the behaviour causing the problem in a simple, straightforward manner and do not allow yourself to become emotional: 'I don't like you to twirl around when we are on the mat and you must answer questions when I ask you.'
- State how you feel but do not involve other people: 'I am worried about your rudeness and I am sad that you feel you can shout out at me.'
- Describe your feelings in simple terms: 'You know our class rule is to be polite to each other at all times. Your shouting makes me feel sad because you know it is not allowed in class.'
- Empathise or show sympathy with the other person's view (without endorsing it): 'I understand that not getting a turn makes you feel upset sometimes.'
- Specify what you would like the child to do and what you will do: 'I want you to stop saying rude things and twirling around on the mat so that I can offer you a turn. I will make sure I do when I see you sitting quietly.'
- Decide what your response to the child's action will be.

Being assertive and identifying a resolution to a problem is very different from being aggressive or belligerent. You should never lose control of your temper in class. If you do, you may make a situation worse and lose authority with the children. However, it is important to be able to appear cross when necessary.

Frequently asked questions

1. 'I have never taught a class of children, or even more than a small group and I know that I have to take whole classes. Suppose they simply won't do what I ask?'

If you approach the class correctly, they will do what you ask. Begin the placement by reading the behaviour policy and observing your teacher. Make absolutely sure you know the whole range of rewards and sanctions so that you can offer these appropriately. Start with a short, carefully planned activity that the children are used to doing, such as reading a story to the class. This will help you to build up your confidence gradually. The most important thing is to appear confident.

2. 'One child in my class is really trying my patience. She interrupts, shouts in class and is openly insolent. Can I send her outside to cool off?'

First of all you need to read your school policy and talk to your teacher. In general, sending children out of the class is not acceptable, as this might put them at risk. In any case, even thinking of this is very extreme and you should have exhausted the whole range of sanctions before you considered a severe measure such as this. Your school will have a procedure for dealing with poor behaviour, such a writing names on the board, keeping children in for five minutes at play and involving other staff. Explore these with the support of your teacher. Finally, remember that you are not alone on placement. To re-establish order in the class, you should ask your teacher to work with you in class and help you to manage this child.

3. 'I have a delightful nursery class. Can I give them sweets to reward good behaviour?'

It is not really a good idea to reward good behaviour with sweets for a number of reasons. The school will have a health education policy that will certainly not include the use of sweets. It would be a shame to undermine early messages about healthy eating by making sweets a reward. You may also find that some children are allergic to certain ingredients commonly found in sweets, such as lactose or nuts or nut derivatives. Finally, many parents would prefer not to have children associate sweets with rewards and to be in control of the sweets their children eat. Instead of sweets, you can use stickers and praise and take the opportunity of fruit time to enjoy eating together.

4. 'One boy in my class is blatantly rude to me and calls out in my lessons. How should I deal with it?'

First, discuss this with the teacher. Does he or she have the same problem and what action has he or she taken? You may want to ask your teacher or mentor to observe a lesson so that you can discuss the behaviour that is troubling you. You must decide, preferably with your mentor, exactly what is and is not acceptable. This will stop you over-reacting.

If the school has established practices, such as writing 'strikes' on the board and adding these up to some other punishment, use these. It is always best to use a system known to the child. You should take the child aside, so that he does not have an audience, and discuss clearly and rationally what is acceptable and unacceptable and how you will treat such behaviour. Make sure you find opportunities to praise the child for his efforts at least as often as you have to reprimand him, as this is one way to develop more acceptable behaviour.

5. 'On Friday the class was really difficult and I just lost my temper and went ballistic. Now I feel embarrassed and I am worried about controlling the class.'

Losing your temper is a sign of desperation and not something you should repeat. You need some support from your mentor or class teacher. Spend a couple of lessons observing how teachers use very small rewards and sanctions (starting with a smile or frown and working up to a sticker or name on a board) before you have a meeting with your mentor. Then review the school policy with the mentor and check you know how to reward and punish in very tiny steps. This is how to keep control of the situation. Are you using time badly, failing to explain tasks or giving children work they cannot do? Discuss this honestly with your mentor and make sure your lessons are well planned with a good pace. This will prevent trouble.

6. **'I am being driven mad by the children in my P4 class. Whenever I ask them to do group or individual tasks they constantly ask trivial questions about where to put dates, what to do with rubbers and how to spell words. They don't do it to the teacher.'**

There are two possibilities here. First of all, you may not be explaining the tasks clearly and failing to refer to the support systems the teacher uses. This may have left the children confused. Check you know how your teacher gives instructions and what usual practice is in terms of dates and finding spellings. Enforce these routines politely but firmly and the children will respond to routines they are used to. The second possibility is that the children have noticed that you do not know their routines and are taking advantage of the situation to put off starting work. The answer is the same – show that you know the routines.

REFLECTIVE TASK

Working with your mentor or class teacher (or even another colleague) audit the positive/negative balance of your responses to children.

Start by compiling a list of all the rewards and sanctions you use. For example:

Rewards

- Smile
- Eye contact
- 'Well done' (praise)

Sanctions

- Ignoring a comment
- Frowning at a child
- Asking someone to sit down/be quiet

Your colleagues can use this list to do a tally chart of your rewards/sanctions in a single lesson. Aim to find out:

- What is the balance of rewards and sanctions in your lesson?
- Who do you give most attention to?
- What can you do to ensure you give more rewards than sanctions, and that this is a calm sensible reward?

Child protection

Children and young people have a fundamental right to be protected from harm and have a right to expect schools to provide a safe and secure environment. It is a guiding principle of the law and child protection procedures that the protection and welfare of the child must always be the first priority. The protection of children and young people is a shared community responsibility and failure to provide an effective response can have serious consequences for the child. Teachers and other education staff are in a unique position to identify and help abused children. Your school will have a child protection policy that you should read.

In a school placement, if you suspect any child is subject to the categories of abuse identified by the Scottish Government document 'Safe and Well' – neglect, physical injury, sexual abuse or emotional abuse, or a child discloses abuse to you, you must follow the school policy and inform the teacher designated responsible (who will be identified in the school policy). This is a highly confidential matter and you should treat it as such. The teacher responsible may choose to share the information with the class teacher but it is not a matter for you to discuss with other staff.

If a child chooses to disclose abuse to you, you should:

- listen to them quietly in privacy but do not interrogate them or ask leading questions;
- make it clear to the child that you cannot keep the information confidential;
- be calm, reassuring and non-judgemental and do not seem to reproach the child, i.e. avoid questions like 'Why didn't you tell...?'
- make a record of what the child has said as soon as you can and date it;
- tell the designated teacher for child protection, preferably on the day the disclosure happens, and pass your notes to him or her.

You can be sure that any allegation of this sort will be dealt with sensitively, swiftly and thoroughly. You may need support yourself to cope with this sort of experience. In the first instance you can get this from your mentor, course tutor or a university counsellor. You can also ring the NSPCC helpline on 0808 800 5000.

A SUMMARY OF **KEY POINTS**

> On professional placement you will work with a range of other adults, including other practitioners, teaching assistants, parents, visiting professionals and administrative staff.

> Working closely with other practitioners and teaching assistants involves understanding their roles and planning carefully for their involvement in all parts of the lesson or session.

> Managing the behaviour of the children you are teaching involves signalling clearly that you are the teacher, know what you are doing, have interesting work and high expectations. Sometimes, this is not as simple as it sounds.

> To take the place of the regular teacher you need to know how the school, class and teacher work. Read the school policy, observe the class and the teacher. Make sure that you know the very fine grading of rewards and sanctions and the teacher's expectations for behaviour.

> Act the part of the teacher. Your body language, how you speak to the children and your apparent confidence, together with well-paced lessons and appropriate activities, will work to ensure an orderly learning environment.

> Your teacher is there to support you. As you gain confidence you will take over managing behaviour in class but you should not be afraid to work closely with the teacher to address particular issues.

> Read the school child protection policy and know who the designated teacher responsible is. If you have any child protection concerns, report to the designated teacher and follow it up with a written, dated report.

Resources

The Learning and Teaching Scotland website has very useful materials on all the issues in this chapter including behaviour management and child protection at http://www.ltscotland.org.uk/ It has a behaviour support toolkit at – http://www.ltscotland.org.uk/inclusiveeducation/images/BehaviourSupportToolkit_tcm4-253377.pdf

The government site specifically dealing with aspects of behaviour management is the Better Behaviour, Better Learning site at http://www.betterbehaviourscotland.gov.uk/

Child protection is dealt with by the government document – 'Safe and Well' which can be found at http://www.scotland.gov.uk/Resource/Doc/57346/0016229.pdf and the role of the teacher in guidance and personal support is dealt with in 'Happy, Safe and Achieving their Potential' at http://www.scotland.gov.uk/Resource/Doc/36496/0023597.pdf

A child friendly summary of the articles from the UN Convention on the Rights of the Child can be found at http://www.sccyp.org.uk/webpages/cypr_rightsofthechild.php on the website of the Scotland's Commissioner for Children and Young People.

Childline Scotland can be found at http://www.childline.org.uk/Scotland.asp

8
Moving on

This chapter offers advice about completion of placements. By the end of the chapter you will know how to:

- **review your progress on placement;**
- **conclude your placement;**
- **prepare for your next stage;**

Reviewing your progress on placement

You will review your progress as you go through your placement but there is a point towards the end of your placement when you should take time to make an overall review. The reasons for this are:

- to check you have done the tasks you had planned and used all the training opportunities on offer;
- to review whether you have met the targets you set for the placement or during the placement;
- to identify progress you have made towards demonstrating the Standards for ITE;
- to decide what constitutes evidence of your progress towards the Standards for ITE and to store this appropriately;
- to prepare for a review meeting with your tutor after your placement to set new targets for future placements or your probationary year.

You might have done some of these things for your mid-placement review with your teacher, if one was planned and held. Before the final week of your placement, revisit your targets and progress so that you are ready for a final meeting with your teacher, mentor or tutor to discuss final reports.

You will have been assessed by your course tutor on a placement visit and the school will write a final report on your progress. You may have an opportunity to discuss the school with your mentor or teacher before you leave. You may want to be prepared for this by having evidence from your file and classwork ready for such a meeting. In this way you can contribute positively to your assessment.

Concluding a placement

The end of placement is an important time for you. It is a goal you have worked hard to achieve but it is also slightly strange for you to be passing the class back to another teacher. A report of some kind will be written about your placement by your class teacher or by your mentor or both together and you will probably have a chance to discuss with them how well you have achieved your targets. You will also be concluding some important relationships. The first of these is the relationship with your class teacher, who will have become used to working closely with you and will now take up the reins of a class who have become used to being taught by both of you. As your placement will probably end before the end of term, your teacher will need to carry on teaching seamlessly when you leave. In the last week of your placement you need to make sure you do the following things.

- Return all the resources you have borrowed. It is very annoying for your teacher to find, a week after you have left, that you have mistakenly retained photocopiable sheets, computer software or teachers guides, etc. Remember to return anything you may have borrowed from other members of staff or from school resources.
- Check that you have all taken your resources and equipment away as it will inconvenience everyone if you have to keep coming back.
- Mark and record all the work the children have done for you. If these are pieces for assessment, ensure they are filed in the right place and correctly annotated.
- Make sure you have all the material you need to complete any assignments that have been set by your tutors. If you need evidence from the children's work, make sure you have asked permission to either photocopy the work or to take the work away with you. If possible, take more examples of work than you think you need if you have not yet written the assignment. It is not usually possible to go back and ask for more examples of work at a later date.
- Have a final tidy up and check that you have replaced all books and resources in the teacher's allocated places and that any activities you have done with the children are tidied away.
- Ensure you pass up-to-date records of the work the children have done with you to your teacher. It is a good idea to arrange a time to discuss the records and to highlight the objectives the children have addressed on the medium-term plan. This, with your records, allows the teacher to take over again smoothly.
- Check that any displays for which you are responsible are complete and labelled.
- Check any outstanding commitments. If you have agreed to come back to help with an assembly or a trip, make sure you know the details before you leave. If you are coming back for another placement later, mention this to your teacher.

Most importantly of all, make sure you thank your teacher explicitly for his or her help and the training they have given you, even if you are coming back to the school or class for a further placement. Make sure this is more than a casual leave-taking: pick out some specific help they have given you and something you have learned from them. Most trainees follow up thanks with a short note or card and in some cases a small gift. The teacher has given you a great deal of time and support and entrusted their class to you. It is rewarding for them to be reminded that you are grateful for this when they are engaged in realigning their work with the class.

If you have worked closely with a mentor you will need similarly to make sure they are aware of your gratitude for their support and time. At some stage they will have a discussion with you about your progress during the placement and this will contribute to a report or profile that assesses your performance against the benchmark standards. Remember to thank your mentor explicitly for the training they have given you in the same way as you would your teacher.

The final report from the school may be completed before you leave the placement and you may be given an opportunity to comment on it. Frequently however, the school completes the report after you have left and posts it to your tutor or university. You should be given a copy of the report when the university receives it.

Finally, when you finish a placement, you need to conclude your relationship with the class. It will have been a very complex, intense and demanding relationship and leaving the children can make you very emotional. The children in your placement class have played a big part in your training and you will remember some of them for the rest of your career. You have some responsibilities towards them as well. You need to make sure you have returned their work and kept any promises you made to them in terms of rewards such as 'Golden Time', exciting games or activities.

The end of the placement is not the time for a sentimental speech, no matter how emotional you might be feeling, but do make sure you explain to the class that you will be leaving them. You should explain this positively so that they understand that this is something you had planned and that you enjoyed your time with them. Pick out some incidents or lessons you have particularly enjoyed and some examples of good classwork or behaviour. You should make it clear that the class teacher will be returning to working with them full time from now on. You might want to put up a poster or card to thank the children for the time you have been working with them.

After leaving a school, you have a duty of confidentiality towards the school, teachers and children. If you use examples of school documents in assignments, you should ask permission from the school and make sure the extract is anonymised. You should not gossip about the school, teachers or the children and if you do use examples of your own experience, or children's work, in the professional setting of your course, you should do so in such a way that the teachers, school or children cannot be identified. This is also important where photos of the school or children have been taken, with the permission of the school.

You may be asked at some stage to complete a Student Evaluation of School Placement. This is a new scheme allowing students to reflect on the experience they have had in a particular school.

The intention of this evaluation is to help schools to improve the quality of the student experience and consists of a set of questions about your placement. Remember where possible to respond positively about your placement and to offer constructive comments. The majority of placement experiences are extremely positive, but occasionally there are issues that leave a student unhappy with the way the placement has gone. Any issues that arise during the placement should be discussed with your tutor at the time and they will advise on the best way to deal with them. Try not to let personal issues such as differences of opinion colour your reflection of the whole school when you complete the evaluation.

Unless this has been your final placement, you will now be returning to university to continue your course or to prepare for the next placement in which case the cycle begins again.

An unsuccessful placement

If you have not achieved the required standard for the placement for whatever reasons, in most cases you will be offered a retrieval placement at some later date (probably at the beginning of the next academic year). This may also be offered to you if you have been unable to complete the placement for whatever reason – for example, ill-health or family issues.

This is a chance for you to gain more experience at this level and to address the weaknesses that were previously identified. You must demonstrate the appropriate attitude and regard this as a chance to further develop your skills and to show that you can achieve the standard. It is important that you read as much as possible and talk to your tutor before going on this placement. Find out exactly what you need to achieve to pass, since in many cases a second failure at this level will have serious consequences for you. Make sure your paperwork is up to standard, neat, well organised and comprehensive. Do some focused reading about the areas where you failed to achieve a satisfactory level and highlight this in your evaluations. Make sure your lesson plan is carefully thought through and your teaching addresses the learning outcomes you have set. When you talk to your tutor after the lesson, be honest and ready to discuss both the positive and negative aspects of your lesson. It is up to you to prove on this placement that you have made the effort to upgrade your knowledge and skills and have addressed former concerns.

If, at the end of the course, you still have an outstanding placement to complete, you will not be able to begin your probation. In this case, if you successfully complete the placement, you will be able to register as a supply teacher and teach until the following year when you will be able to take up a probationary placement. You may choose to undertake all your probation as a supply teacher. This will be dealt with in the next chapter.

Final placement

If this was the final placement of your course then the last weeks on campus will be spent focusing on the next steps you will be taking. Some establishments use this time to bring in a number of external speakers who will give you information and suggestions to help with this. Some bring back former students from a previous year to talk about their first year in class. Other lectures may be given by university staff. There is much important information and help to be gained from these 'induction' sessions and it is important not to miss them. In most cases, attendance will not be optional and may be a prerequisite for graduation.

Profile for entry to the teaching profession

You will be asked in the final weeks to complete a personal statement for your final profile. This is the document that will be sent to the school in which you will undertake your probation year. The document is in several parts:

- One section will give details of your academic profile from your course, e.g. marks for exams and assignments.
- Your tutor will complete a personal profile report in which they will take into consideration all the reports from school placements – both those from tutors and from the schools involved; information from tutors on the courses you have completed and their own knowledge of you personally.
- You will complete a personal statement which includes your targets for the future and a statement of your commitment to teaching and the skills and personal qualities you bring.

You will receive instructions on the best way to complete your statement and should have a chance to see and discuss what your tutor has written and to comment on this although it will not necessarily be changed as a result of your comments.

Provisional registration with the GTCS

Forms for this are usually sent out by the GTCS before Christmas in the academic year in which you are likely to graduate. They will be issued to you along with instructions for completion and a date for return – usually again before the Christmas break. It is really important that you return the forms on time.

The form will ask you where you would prefer to be allocated a probation placement. The selection will not be of an individual school but the selection of a local authority. You can nominate a number authorities in which you would be prepared to work. There is no guarantee that you will be allocated a placement in your first choice of authority or near to where you live or will be living. Local authorities providing placements usually try to allocate places that are within reasonable travel distance of a given address but this cannot be guaranteed and you will not be given a choice of locations. Think carefully about your choices. If you are considering taking a placement far from your home, friends and family then think this through from all angles – travel, accommodation, self-sufficiency, social life, etc. Joining a small rural community, perhaps on an island, far from home sounds magical and can be a wonderful experience but can be very lonely at times if you are used to being part of a large group of friends and/or family. On the other hand, this may be just the adventure you are waiting for.

Places are allocated by local authority staff and schools do not usually have a choice about the probationers they take. You will be advised further about the procedure by your university.

Completed forms are used to determine how many placements each local authority will need to find and how much funding will be needed to cover this. Schools need as much notice as possible of impending probationer places in order to plan teaching arrangements for the following year, but will not be informed of the names of probationers until near the end of the summer term.

It is only at this stage that the real uptake of places will be known, since some students may leave the course or need further placements before they reach the required standard and so will not be able to take up a probation placement that year. Students are usually notified of their placement school in June, before the end of the school term.

You will be told when you may contact the school to which you have been assigned. Initial contact by phone is the best approach. Most schools will then invite you to visit before the end of term and some may be in a position to show you your new classroom and to talk about your new class. Use this opportunity to find out as much as possible, including times when you may have access to your classroom at the beginning of the new term.

Resources

The GTCS website has a student section where you can ask for a provisional registration form in cases where for some reason your University has not supplied you with one. Find it at www.gtcs.org.uk/Registration/student_information.asp This page also explains how to change your selection of local authorities if your form has already been handed in and you have changed your mind about where you would like to work.

9
Your probation year

This chapter explains the next steps in becoming a fully qualified teacher in Scotland and offers advice about your first teaching experiences. By the end of the chapter you will have a clearer understanding of induction, of the pathways to full registration and the demands that will be made on you during this process. You will also know how to:

- **review your progress during your induction year;**
- **be successful as a supply teacher before and after induction;**
- **begin to look for a teaching post.**

Achieving the Standard for Full Registration (SFR)

In Scotland, teachers who have achieved provisional registration with the GTCS by completing successfully a course at university and school experience move into a probationary period which must be completed satisfactorily to achieve full registration as a teacher.

Prior to 2001, this was achieved by completing the equivalent of two years of teaching and receiving satisfactory reports at the end of both the first and second years. Although this worked for most it was on a 'sink-or-swim' basis and some probationers on either long-term or short-term supply contracts had little or no targeted support, continuity or assessed teaching. When the McCrone Agreement was introduced in 2001, it brought with it a commitment to providing a guaranteed induction year in a selected school for all probationers. For those not able to take up this induction year for whatever reason, the alternative pathway of achieving the SFR through supply teaching still remains.

The final goal is to achieve the SFR – to become a fully qualified teacher. As with the standard for ITE, this is achieved by attaining a set of benchmark standards. These can be found on the GTCS website and echo those attained in achieving provisional registration.

The Standards are in three inter-related categories as before:

- professional knowledge and understanding;
- professional skills and abilities;
- professional values and personal commitment.

The attainment of these Standards takes place almost entirely in school and the judgement of success or failure rests with the school to a certain extent since they write the reports upon which the probationer is judged. The Standards provide a clear and concise description of the baseline professional standards for a fully qualified teacher and apply not only to new teachers but to all qualified teachers throughout their careers. In setting down the qualities, knowledge, skills and values that a qualified teacher should demonstrate, the aim is to ensure consistency – everyone can be judged against the Standards regardless of the circumstances under which they train or work.

The bridge between ITE and the probationary year is the profile produced at the end of ITE. This provides a record of achievement that travels with the probationer and also contains indications of the strengths and development needs of the probationer, giving guidance for the start for the probationary year.

The Teacher Induction Scheme

The scheme, set up as a result of the McCrone Report, is called the Teacher Induction Scheme (TIS). Its aim is to offer probationary teachers a year in a school where they will be supported and mentored, be given structured training and regular review in order to meet the SFR.

This scheme has proved very successful both from the trainee point of view, providing support and encouragement during the challenging first year of teaching, and from the school's point of view, bringing new ideas and energy to the school. The posts are funded to some extent by the government and may allow schools to increase their staffing levels for the time the probationer is with them.

At the end of the Teacher Induction Scheme probationary teachers are eligible to apply for full registration as a teacher with the GTCS. The assessment will be based on interim and final reports from the school in which induction has been completed.

The GTCS document 'Achieving the Standard for Full Registration' gives the following information regarding eligibility for TIS:

> *Eligibility is normally restricted to those students graduating from a Scottish Higher Education Institution with a Teaching Qualification whose training has been publicly funded. This includes students from other parts of the UK and other parts of the EU provided they have been assessed as eligible for Home Fees. This is regardless of how these fees are funded, i.e. through SAAS, Local Education Authorities, self-funded, Northern Ireland Education and Library Boards, etc. Students who pay overseas or full fees are not in publicly-funded places and are therefore not eligible to join the Scheme.*

The aims of induction

Draper and O'Brien (2006) suggest that the aim of induction is to 'help people settle into a new work setting' but in terms of teaching it is usually thought of as development towards achieving the SFR, although in reality for probationary teachers it is both.

The GTCS lists the following as the aims of induction for the probationary teacher to be:

- further development of professional knowledge and understanding of the relevant areas of the primary curriculum;
- to ensure a broad understanding of the education system, policy and practice and their role within it;
- to encourage articulation of professional values and practices and to link this to theoretical perspectives and principles;
- to further develop the ability to plan, implement and evaluate teaching programmes and learning appropriate to the needs of the children;
- to extend and enhance the range of teaching and learning strategies;

- to encourage co-operative working with other professionals and adults;
- to further develop classroom management and organisation skills including effective behaviour management;
- to consolidate understanding and skills in assessment, recording and reporting and use the assessment to enhance the teaching and learning;
- to further develop critical reflection and to take personal responsibility for their own professional development.

Most of these build on the skills, attitudes and values, knowledge and understanding developed during ITE, some will be consolidated and others developed further. This view of the induction year shows it to be a time of 'proving competence or developing practice which links to a prescribed pattern of practice and developing as a teacher' (Draper and O'Brien, 2006). From this perspective, it is a time in which to further develop as a teacher and to prove that you can 'do the job'.

As a probationer, from your point of view, there is also the 'settling in' aspect to consider. In most cases the year will be spent in a school in which you have not previously taught.

'Settling in' will entail a similar experience to that of placement. You will get to know the people you will be working with – firstly the staff and then the children in the class. You will need to know how that particular school works – what systems are in place for daily routines, such as lunch arrangements, registers, absences, behaviour management, and you will need to establish clearly what is expected of you in terms of your teaching commitment, assessment, evaluation, training, recording, etc. Geographical knowledge of what and who are to be found where, along with the best sources of help and information, will allow you to function efficiently. Remember, every school has its own characteristics and will be different to every other school.

Some of this information can be obtained before you begin your induction year. Usually you will able to contact and visit your new school at the end of the previous summer term and so can spend some time planning for and learning about your new post. The school might have an information booklet or package ready for you. Use the model from your student school placement file to find out about school policies, layout, etc., and have all this information in a file ready to help you at the beginning of term.

The nature of induction

The nature of induction year relies on three main participants.

The school

The school in which you will teach for your induction year will have been selected by the local authority as one that can provide a suitable environment and support for a probationer. It must have suitably qualified and experienced staff to support you and to be able to provide effective monitoring and evaluation as you progress through the year. It must be able to provide a suitable classroom experience in which your skills as a teacher can be developed.

The school will have arranged for you to teach a class for 70 per cent of the normal contact time for a class teacher. A fully registered class teacher has 22.5 hours class contact time and so you will have 15.75 hours with your class each week. This means that you will have around three half-days out of class in which to undertake professional development. The time out of class is not intended to be spent marking or preparing lessons unless for a detailed evaluation of how the pupils' needs are being met and how progress is being made towards SFR.

In some instances, where schools are allocated several probationers, it may be necessary for you to share a class with another probationer and spend the rest of your allocated teaching time with a different class. This has become unavoidable in some schools where circumstances such as a lack of available staff or suitable classes make it impossible to give each probationer their own class. The GTCS advice is that in this situation, you should spend at least 0.55 FTE with one class.

There are considerable implications for a school arranging to have a probationary teacher, not least providing a mentor who will be able to spend time with the probationer and another teacher to teach the class when the probationer is not teaching. Add to this provision of cover for all the other teachers to have their 'McCrone time' and it can be seen that there can be serious organisational challenges, particularly in a small school. Be prepared to be flexible.

The mentor/supporter

The school will provide a mentor or dedicated supporter who will work with you throughout the year. This will be an experienced teacher with whom you will be able to have regular meetings and be able to talk to about any issues with which you are having problems. They will watch you teach from time to time and provide feedback to help you improve and deal with any issues.

You will be working closely with this teacher and it is important that you establish a good working relationship within which you are comfortable asking questions and seeking advice and from whom you can accept feedback and suggestions for improvement. You must be prepared to take responsibility for your development and not rely too heavily on your supporter. You must also take the advice you are given and act on it. Other members of staff may be involved in this process.

The probationer

Your role throughout this year is to act as a full member of staff with all the responsibilities that that entails and to be actively contributing to school life. You will be expected to act as a teacher in a professional manner with due consideration for confidentiality, support and welfare of the children in the school, respect for school rules and standards, etc. You will be responsible for the teaching and learning that occurs in your lessons and you will maintain recording and reporting procedures. You will have responsibilities regarding resources in your classroom and in maintaining required school standards of dress and attendance. Your duties may include school trips and other activities that take you out of the classroom. You will be expected to attend in-service days and take part in staff development, to work with other professionals such as classroom assistants, ASL staff, psychologists, social workers, etc., as required. As a class teacher you will be expected to attend such things as stage meetings and working groups and will be responsible for report writing and reporting to parents for your class.

During this year, you will begin to establish your own identity as a teacher. Although you are required to achieve a specific set of targets you will already be aware that every teacher has their own way of doing this and their own style of teaching and management of the class. During your previous placements, you were in someone else's class and needed to fit in with them to a certain extent. This is the first time you will be able to explore your own style and identity although you must keep within acceptable practice in the school – a very noisy art lesson might be a wonder of creative expression but you may get into trouble if it disturbs everyone else. You will need to reach a comfortable working arrangement with another teacher or probationer who will be taking your class when you are involved in CPD. Be prepared to be creative along the lines suggested by your lectures and reading – you will make mistakes and should learn from them but you will also learn how to manage innovative approaches and make them successful learning experiences. Discuss your ideas with your mentor, who should be able to advise you how to make them successful and meaningful learning experiences.

The induction year should be a time of intense professional development for you that includes the following:

- Time spent teaching – taking on the full role of class teacher with responsibility for most curriculum areas, layout of the room, pastoral care of pupils, etc. This is only a 70 per cent commitment and so will inevitably involve working with another teacher or teachers in a 'job-share' style of role.
- Observed sessions/supporter meetings – regular meetings with your mentor/supporter that give you time for discussion and feedback from observed sessions. Other members of staff such as members of the senior management team may also observe your lessons and give you feedback.
- CPD experiences, including courses run by the local authority especially for probationary teachers; courses run by other providers for teachers in general; team-teaching in other areas of the school; experiences such as working with ASL teachers or spending time in an attached nursery or local secondary school.

The GTCS document 'Achieving the Standard for Full Registration' (available on the GTCS website) gives in some detail the roles of individuals involved in the induction process and you should read this before beginning your placement.

What to expect in your induction year

Before you arrive

Although you will be in need of a holiday once your course finishes, you will probably find that after a break, you are ready to think of the next steps.

Before the start of your first term, you should be able to go into your new classroom and get the room and your resources prepared. Some preparation can be done at home if your time in school before the children return is going to be limited.

- Prepare class lists with boxes for ticks on the computer – these could include lists of reading groups for assessment, for marking reading to be done and completed, etc.
- Design a reading record cover and a folder to keep reading records in.
- Decide on an activity to start your first day – try not to make it an essay on 'What I did in the holidays', Try to think of an activity that will help you to get to know the children and let them know what kind of teacher you intend to be. Remember to set rules for behaviour and give careful instructions.
- Plan some general revision lessons in maths – as interactive as possible. Children's minds need to be brought back up to speed when they come back after a long break and before you launch into the maths

scheme, it is good to spend a few sessions on revision.

- The first afternoon needs a good activity to get everyone going again – this might need to become a short topic that lasts just the first week before other subjects will be ready to go. You could pose a problem and work with the children to find a solution – e.g. you need to find a way to identify them all while you get to know their names. If they move seats for different activities, their 'identifiers' will need to move with them. Perhaps they could come up with a novel solution – paper bracelets or 'bands', names on clothes pegs, etc. Turn it into a design task and then make them.
- Think how you are going to organise the classroom (if you have control of this) and where you will seat each child. Where will you put the maths equipment, etc.? Think what you might want to put up on the walls – perhaps you could design some maths reminder cards, e.g. words meaning 'add', words meaning 'subtract', times tables. Where will you display the class rules and what will they look like? Will you have a points scheme? Make a list of resources to check – scissors, glue, paints, paintbrushes.
- You might think of 'early finisher' activities to go in a wallet on the wall – some poetry cards, language cards, maths puzzles, etc., can all be made up on the computer before you go into school.
- You might want to choose a class story to begin on your first day – perhaps some activities in the first week could be linked to this.
- Set up your CPD portfolio (see under 'Working through the year').

Try to think through as much of your first week as you can – there will be a huge amount of information to take in and you need to have as much as possible prepared earlier. Some of the activities you made or used on your placements might come in useful here – particularly if they went well.

In your profile you will have highlighted areas for development – this might be a time when you could do some reading to support this.

Before the children come back to school

Once you are able to go into the classroom, begin to arrange the furniture and try out some ideas. You might want to consider the following.

- Remember to allow space for bags and for movement.
- Once you put the chairs and tables where you think they should go, move around the room and try out different positions – can you see clearly? Does looking at the board involve turning around? Is there room to move your chair out easily?
- Have you allowed space somewhere to gather the class together for more involved discussion and teaching?
- Have you got space for different areas within the class – a table to hear reading groups and work closely with small groups? Have you room for a writing table, spelling base, library corner, etc.?
- Where will you have your desk – will it be in front traditionally so that you can sit and mark, etc., while the children are working? Will it be flat against the wall because you need the space and won't be sitting in it in school time?
- Where will the children collect jotters from and leave books for marking?
- Will you have a noticeboard for the children to display important information and things they want to display such as certificates, photos, etc.? Will you have a question board where you can post a question and the children can leave their answers on sticky notes?
- Have you a space to display WALT and WILF?
- Do you want to have a small board on which to work with groups?
- Will you be using an interactive whiteboard? Is there space to bring it in if it is a mobile board?
- Where will packed lunches go?

- In most classrooms there will be decisions to be made about the types of jotters you will need – where do you find them? Is there a school policy on the types of jotters used for each subject? You might want to use a piece of coloured insulating tape on the spines of jotters to make them readily identified – particularly for subjects which involve groups – a different colour for each group makes it easy to pick their jotters out of a pile.
- Where will resources be stored – pencils, erasers, felt pens, rulers, paints, paint brushes, etc.? Are you going to have a container on each table to hold essentials? How will the children sharpen pencils – over the bin or into a tub on each table?
- How will you organise art activities – where will paintings dry? How can art resources be arranged for easy access? How will you arrange washing up and tidying? Do you need to post instructions on the wall for this?
- Are you going to have group names – how will you decide on them? Will you have signs on tables or hanging from the ceiling? Do you need to make up points charts, group charts, places to list group tasks for maths/language, etc.?
- Do you need a box to store jewellery to take up to the gym for PE?
- Do you need a box with small cards with the children's names so that tasks, duties, etc., can be allocated fairly by taking the next name out of the box?
- Do you have all your resources ready for the first day and underway for the rest of the week?
- Do you know what the class routines will be – these may be up to you or part of the school ethos. For example, how do children come in in the morning? Where to they leave coats, bags, shoes? Is there a school timetable or is it up to you? When will you have time in the gym?
- Familiarise yourself with the textbooks and resources for all the subjects you will be teaching.

In the first few days, before the children return to school, you will probably have meetings with the head teacher, your mentor and the person who will be sharing your class. You might find it helpful to think about things you need to know before you have these meetings – how will work be divided between yourself and the other teacher? What are the school routines for lunches, absences, registration, etc.?

Make notes at all these meeting so that you have everything written down – there is too much to take in otherwise. Make a list of the staff members and their roles as you learn them, so that you will know who to ask or who to send children to for specific things.

Make sure you go over all the decisions you have made about your classroom with your mentor. You might not be free to make all of the above decisions, particularly since you will be working with another teacher – whether another probationer or an experienced teacher. In this case you will need to reach an agreement or compromise on the layout and routines. It is important that when a class has two teachers, they work together to find solutions that suit both of them. You cannot expect children to follow one set of routines for part of the week and do things differently for the rest of the week.

When the children arrive

They will be excited to be back and curious about you. Follow your carefully made plan – make sure you get a chance to hear any news they have about what they have been doing – better to get it out of the way and it will give you time to learn something about them. Find a way of allowing them to introduce themselves and tell you a little about the things they like/ dislike or are good at or hobbies, etc. Remember that this class does not yet have set routines – you need to teach these and in these first few days will need to focus on reinforcing the behaviour you are expecting, the school rules and the way you want things done.

Don't introduce too much all at once – some routines can wait a few days. You might use the first day to discuss class rules and decide what they should be – better if the children are involved in this process. Remember you have to teach the rules and what they mean and always refer to them when dealing with misdemeanours.

In the first week, you will discover how things work, problems, things you've forgotten and things that are really good. As you get to know your class and the staff around you, you will be able to feel more relaxed. Remember the things you learned and did as a student – take ideas from your own activities and things you saw teachers doing that you thought were good. Before you know it you will have settled into the routine and the first week will be past.

Working through the year

The GTCS document 'Achieving the Standard for Full Registration' gives a description of the induction year in terms of your development. It guides you through the early sessions in terms of induction by the school, induction by your employer, i.e. the local authority, discussion with your mentor/supporter and developing an Initial Development Action Plan – looking at your profile, identifying your initial development needs and proposed focus for development in the first term.

Throughout the term you will be engaged in CPD activities in your time out of class. There will be regular meetings arranged by the local authority. The local authority will have appointed an induction co-ordinator to whom you will be introduced early in the session. The co-ordinator is responsible for overseeing placements and advising schools and probationers about any issues that arise through the year. They are responsible for arranging a series of probationer meetings at which you will get a chance to meet up and share experiences with other probationers and usually will have a chance to request particular topics for study. Some sessions will be undertaken as a group with the co-ordinator focusing on a particular aspect of CPD; some sessions involve external presenters to deliver CPD on an area of their expertise.

During your time out of class, you may also be sent on courses from other providers and attended by experienced teachers. You may engage on some focused reading, working with specific teachers in the school, etc. Regular meetings with your supporter will deliver feedback and next steps and give you a chance to discuss how things are going with your class. You are expected to take a proactive role in this and maintain ongoing self-evaluation and reflection.

You must keep a portfolio to record the CPD undertaken and your reflections on your development as well as notes of meetings with your supporter and evidence of your success. You should keep a note of the observed lessons that you have delivered and the feedback you were given. The portfolio is your record of what you have done towards your achieving SFR and should have your Action Plan and the steps you have taken along it. You will need to keep this up to date as it will provide the basis for your review meetings and may be helpful in obtaining a job when you have achieved SFR.

The GTCS suggests that your portfolio should include:

1. your Self-Evaluation Overview and Initial Teacher Education Profile;
2. the Professional Development Action Plan (PDAP) allowing you to identify CPD

requirements;

3. CPD Tracking Record plus any additional details regarding CPD experiences you have undertaken and your evaluation of them;
4. supporter meeting notes;
5. observed teaching feedback;
6. supporting evidence, discussed in how to meet the SFR, including plans and materials used during observed teaching sessions and in other CPD experience;
7. a copy of your Interim Report (at the end of your second term, or equivalent) or Final Report (at the end of your fourth term, or equivalent).

The GTCS recommends that you are observed for five lessons in this first period, each with an agreed focus for observation and discussion. In addition you will have an observed session with someone other than your supporter.

In December, there will be a more formal review meeting with your supporter, head teacher and the other observer. At this meeting, your progress so far will be reviewed with strengths and weaknesses identified and discussed. A Professional Development Action Plan for the next session will be agreed upon. Either during this meeting or afterwards the Interim Profile will be completed. You will have some input in this along with your supporter and the head teacher. This profile will be sent to the GTCS and will be used in making a final decision on your full registration.

The second half of the year will follow a similar pattern, with four observed sessions. The final progress review meeting should be held in late May/early June with a similar agenda to the previous one. At this meeting the final profile will be considered and written and then submitted to the GTCS. If all is satisfactory, the award of Full Registration should follow.

If at any stage of the induction year the school feels that there are problems with your placement or concerns about your attitude, teaching or any other aspect of your placement, they will contact the induction co-ordinator and steps will be taken to address the issues.

You will be given support and help to overcome difficulties – a lot of effort and money has been spent getting you this far in the process and it is in everyone's interest for you to succeed. You must however be proactive – your career is at stake and you must do every-thing you can to achieve success. You must take the advice given and be seen to be acting on it.

At the end of the year

The post is only for one year and it can be difficult emotionally to accept this and be ready to apply for jobs and look for a new position when you feel a part of this school. As with the end of a placement, remember to thank the staff, your mentor/supporter and head teacher for their help and support and follow the same routine as you did on student placement – remember to return materials and books you have borrowed, leave records up to date, etc.

The section at the end of this chapter discusses applying for jobs once you achieve full registration.

If for some reason you chose to withdraw from the scheme – perhaps you find that you are unable to make a full-time commitment for example – you may continue training via the alternative pathway, working as a supply teacher towards the SFR (see section below). In this situation, you have a time limit of three years to complete your training. The GTCS will advise you of the requirements in this situation.

Despite success at ITE level, you may fail to achieve the SFR in this year and there can be serious consequences for doing so although concerns will have been raised throughout the year and action taken to help you overcome problems. It is important to maintain the effort and level of study you put into your ITE training throughout this probationary year. The onus is on you to work to improve your skills and make the most of the experiences offered to you – it is essential that you enter this year motivated, committed and focused as you were for your previous school placements.

Alternative pathways

Late attainment of Provisional Registration

If for some reason you do not achieve Provisional Registration in time to take up a place on the TIS – perhaps you needed an extra placement, have to resit a module or have family circumstances that prevent you beginning in August – you will be able to work as a supply teacher for the remainder of the year until you can rejoin the TIS the following August. You might alternatively choose to continue on supply and complete your probation through supply teaching (see below).

You need to keep the GTCS informed of your plans or circumstances so that a place can be made available for you. You will be given guidance by your university and the GTCS. If this is your situation, refer to the 'Supply teaching' section in this chapter for some suggestions on making this a productive experience. You will not be eligible to apply for permanent council supply posts but will be able to join the register of supply teachers for short-term and occasional contracts.

Probation through supply teaching

If for some reason you chose to not to undertake your probation through the TIS – if, for example you are only able to work part-time or need to be more flexible to suit childcare provision or family demands, or want to work in the independent sector or outside of Scotland – you can complete your probation working as a supply teacher. The requirements are that you need to teach for at least 270 days or four terms and you have a time limit of five years to fulfil this. In exceptional circumstances the GTCS may grant an extension to the period of provisional registration. If the teaching you do is on very short contracts, e.g. a day here and there, you may need to teach for more than 270 days in order to gain enough experience to be successful.

Undertaking your induction through this route means that you work:

- full time or part time on short-term temporary contracts as a supply teacher; or
- on a long-term contract in an independent school; or
- outside of Scotland.

You can download a form from the GTCS website on which you must record all the periods of teaching that you complete.

Record of Teaching Service								
Name and type of School	Employing Authority	Period From	Served To	Full-time/ Part-time		Stages Taught	Certified Correct (HT's Signature)	Date of Interim Submission to GTC Scotland
				F/t	P/t%			

(Additional Record of Teaching Service Sheets are available from www.gtcs.org.uk)

If you are on a long-term contract, you should be able to access targeted CPD that is offered by the local authority to probationers on the TIS but make sure you ask for this from the management in the school. You should always make sure the school knows you are a probationer – that might mean you get more support than an experienced teacher would be given. If you are to be in a school for a long time, the school might arrange for an experienced teacher to mentor you. You will not have an entitlement to time out of class as a TIS probationer. The school will be able to write your interim or final reports if you have been there for a while and have completed the requisite number of days – around 135 days and 270 days respectively. Make sure that the above form is signed at the end of each teaching contract. For example, if you have a contract for six months and it is then renewed for a further four, get it signed at the end of the first contract and again at the end of the second.

If you are on short-term contracts, it is essential that you get this form signed every time you complete a teaching session whether half a day or more. Once you have a filled page, send it in to the GTCS (remember to keep a photocopy). Getting interim and final reports written is more difficult – you may find that you spend more time in one school than others and should ask the head teacher in that school for advice about mentoring and reporting. It may be that that school will support you to some extent in the periods in which you work for them and might be willing to write reports for you when the time comes.

Wherever you are working for your probation, you should contact the induction co-ordinator in the local authority in which you are working or in which you are doing most work and let them know your position. You are entitled to the same CPD provided by the local authority as TIS probationers but you have to make sure that the LA are aware of your position. The induction co-ordinator will be able to advise you on your position regarding time out of school to attend – you will probably have to attend in your own time. You will need to be much more proactive than if you were on a TIS. There will probably not be a team support-ing you and evaluating you regularly so you will need to use all your skills in self-evaluation and research and read to improve your teaching. If you are settled in one school for a while, you might ask for or be offered observation and feedback from the head teacher or another experienced teacher. Make the most of every opportunity and keep a portfolio of your experiences, CPD, etc., as if you were on the TIS. Your portfolio in this case should also contain details of relevant supply days/short-term temporary service, accumulated through your teaching service contributing to your CPD experiences and evidencing your teaching practice.

The GTCS website offers specific guidance to you on this route to SFR: www.gtcs.org.uk/ InformationforProbationersmicrosite/AlternativeRoute/Alternative_Route_guidance.asp

Reviewing your progress during your probation year

Achieving success in ITE will have been a demanding process but is just the first stage in your development as a teacher. The government is committed to encouraging lifelong learning and this is especially relevant to teachers at all stages in their careers. You will have been encouraged to develop as a reflective teacher – one who constantly reviews their performance, skills and needs. The evaluation process that was a requirement of your ITE training should now become your natural practice. Although you will no longer be writing regular evaluations of your lessons, you should still be doing this mentally – identifying strengths and weaknesses and seeking ways of improving areas in which you are less secure. Remember to maintain the cycle illustrated in Figure 9.1.

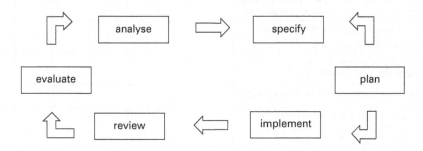

Figure 9.1. Evaluation cycle

The GTCS suggests the following:

- analyse the different approaches to learning and teaching appropriate to the pupils and the community to which they belong;
- specify or define what aspect(s) of learning and teaching are going to be addressed and what it is hoped will be achieved;
- plan what the starting point is and how this approach will be implemented and monitored;
- implement and track the teaching and learning, sharing the work in which you are involved with your supporter and other colleagues, welcoming feedback;
- review what has been achieved;
- evaluate learning, record and identify next steps.

This cycle probably echoes that which you used in your ITE. It is a continuous, everyday process and allows you to reflect on your teaching and to make improvements as you go along.

The process you will follow with your mentor will involve use of the self-evaluation overview – see below. This is available on the GTCS website www.gtcs.org.uk/Informationfor Probationersmicrosite/induction_year_guidance/RecordingEvidence/Self_Evaluation_Overview.asp

	Strengths	Resulting Development Priority			
		High	Med	Low	On-going
Professional Skills and Abilities					
Teaching and Learning:					
are able to plan coherent, progressive and stimulating teaching programmes which match their pupils' needs and abilities, and they can justify what they teach					
communicate clearly making skilful use of a variety of media, and interact productively with pupils, individually and collectively					
use a range of teaching strategies and resources which they can evaluate and justify in terms of curriculum requirements and of the needs and abilities of their pupil					
set and maintain expectations and pace of work for all pupils					
work co-operatively with other professionals, staff and parents					
Classroom Organisation and Management:					
organise and manage classes and resources to achieve safe, orderly and purposeful activity					
manage pupil behaviour and classroom incidents fairly, sensitively and consistently, making sensible use of rewards and sanctions, and seeking and using the advice of colleagues when necessary					
Assessment of Pupils:					
understand and apply the principles of assessment, recording and reporting					
use the results of assessment to evaluate and improve their teaching, and the learning and attainment of the children they teach					
Professional Reflection and Communication:					
learn from their experience of practice and from critical evaluation of relevant literature in their professional development					
convey an understanding of practice and general educational matters in their professional dialogue and communication					
reflect on and act to improve their own professional practice, contribute to their own professional development, and engage in the process of curriculum development					

Professional Knowledge and Understanding					
Curriculum:					
have detailed knowledge and understanding of the relevant areas of the pre-school, primary or secondary school curriculum					
have sufficient knowledge and understanding to fulfil their responsibilities for cross-curricular themes including citizenship, creativity, enterprising attitudes, literacy and numeracy; personal, social and health education; and ICT. (As appropriate to the sector and stage of development)					
demonstrate the knowledge and understanding to enable them to plan coherent and progressive teaching programmes, and justify what they teach					
understand the nature of the curriculum and its development					
Education Systems and Professional Responsibilities:					
have a broad, critical understanding of the principal features of the education system, educational policy and practice, and of their part in it					
have detailed working knowledge of their sector, of the school(s) in which they teach, and of their professional responsibilities within them					
Principles and Perspectives:					
articulate their professional values and practices and relate them to theoretical principles and perspectives					
have research-based knowledge relating to learning and teaching and a critical appreciation of the contribution of research to education in general					
Professional Values and Personal Commitment					
show in their day-to-day practice a commitment to social justice, inclusion and caring for and protecting children					
take responsibility for their professional learning and development					
value, respect and are active partners in the communities in which they work					

In your first meeting with your mentor, you will transfer your strengths from your ITE profile onto the self-evaluation overview and then decide with your mentor what your development priorities will be for each area. This should make obvious the choice of development priorities for the first period from August to December and these should be entered onto the CPD tracking record as follows:

Professional Standard	Reason for choice	Issues for discussion with supporter	Date

Progress made			Sources of evidence
Date/s discussed with Supporter			Further information and guidance
Dates of associated classroom observation visit/s			

Using this form, you should decide which aspect you will focus on first. Concentrate your CPD on addressing this area and improving your practice in the classroom in this area. Record your progress on this form and where the evidence can be found, e.g. your forward plans, children's work, wall display.

So for example, if you decide that improving your behaviour management is your first priority because you are finding this a challenge in your classroom, you might read about assertive discipline in the book by Canter and Canter (2001) and try out their ideas in your class. You might find extra help on the Better Behaviour Better Learning website (www.betterbehaviourscotland.gov.uk) and that might lead you to specific action for certain children. You would record the reading and research you had done in the 'progress made' box. Your mentor might think that you would benefit from a CPD course and you would include that too. Your evidence for improvement might be numeric – the number of times you have to ask for help with behaviour might decrease significantly, certain children may not be in trouble as often as they were, etc. The GTCS site contains more detailed information.

These forms should help you to monitor your progress clearly and your portfolio should also contain samples of work, photographs, etc., as evidence.

Once fully qualified as a teacher, your folio will be the basis for your continuing professional development as a qualified teacher. Current teaching conditions contain a requirement for all teachers to complete 39 hours of CPD per year and to maintain a personal portfolio of their CPD throughout their careers.

Interim and final profiles

These profiles will be completed by your head teacher and your mentor/supporter. They will chart the activities and progress you have made while in your induction year or probationary period. Some parts of the profile will be completed by you – a list of meetings held with your mentor, your weekly timetable, information about your observed teaching sessions and the range of CPD experiences in which you have taken part. The targets you agree with your mentor will also appear – on the interim form your targets for the period to December will be given along with your proposed targets for January to June. The head teacher and your mentor will fill in the other sections detailing the progress you have made and their recommendations to the GTCS. The profiles are to be completed online and you can find them and more detailed instructions for their completion on the GTCS website. The profile must be printed and you must sign it to say that you have read it before it is submitted. In signing, you are not saying that you agree with what it says.

If a satisfactory interim report is submitted to the GTCS then at the end of the probationary period, only the final profile needs to be completed and submitted. If the first interim report highlights some causes for concern or is gives an unsatisfactory grade then another interim report will be submitted at the end of the spring term giving you the chance to address the concerns raised.

When you are recommended for full registration by the school, it is recognition by your peers that you have 'made the grade' – it is the school's recommendation that is upheld by the GTCS.

If at any stage you are having difficulties, it is important to raise your concerns with your mentor – the sooner problems are identified, the sooner action can be taken to help remedy the situation.

Successful supply teaching

The guidance given here will apply to anyone who is working as a supply teacher before beginning TIS; working as a supply teacher through all or part of their probation or who has obtained SFR and has not been successful in obtaining a permanent post.

Teaching in Scotland has always been variable – from time to time there are shortages of teachers and, at other times, too many teachers. If there is a glut of teachers when you qualify, then you will most likely need to work as a supply teacher until the balance is restored and permanent posts become available. Government policy, the age profile of the workforce, class sizes, population trends, etc., all affect the supply of jobs. Most teachers obtain a permanent or long-term supply post within two or three years of qualifying and almost all will be employed for most of the time. The more flexible you can be in terms of availability, the role you are willing to play and location, the easier it will be to find work.

Being a supply teacher may seem daunting and not what you were looking forward to, but will give you some excellent experiences both positive and negative and is a very good grounding for the rest of your career. Although there are drawbacks in terms of uncertainty and challenge, there are advantages in sounding out schools where you might want to become a permanent teacher, being able to impress prospective head teachers, trying out new ways of doing things and being a different sort of teacher for a week knowing that you will walk away and probably not be back in that class again. You may:

- experience a whole range of school environments from excellent to not so good;
- see every type of class arrangement possible;
- have the chance to work in an open-plan or semi-open plan as well as large and small classrooms in old and new schools;
- meet teachers of every type and interact in a number of staffrooms;
- see specialists take lessons across a range of subjects;
- teach children with a range of special needs both with and without support;
- take every type of class imaginable – small, large, quiet, lively, challenging, wonderful, composite, multi-cultural, denominational, etc. As a supply teacher on a short contract, you may be able to work in a denominational school without being approved by the Catholic Church.

Being successful as a supply teacher requires some careful planning and thought, as it does for being a successful class teacher in a more permanent role. The challenges can be different, however, and you need to be prepared.

How it works

Supply teaching is as varied as any other type of teaching. Contracts are usually given out by local authorities (LAs), who will require you to register on their supply list and then will notify you when a vacancy arises. You may be notified by phone or increasingly these days by an automatically generated text message or email. You can register with more than one LA if you are within reach. You may need to supply bank details when you register in order to be paid.

In some cases, you may want to leave a business card with local schools (not a CV), who may then call on you if they are able, to come at short notice. You may have days when there is no work and other times when you are offered more than you can manage. You need to be prepared to work at short notice – half an hour in some cases.

Contracts can vary.

- Short term – half-days to two or three weeks, often to cover teachers who have become ill or who are absent for some other reason, or who are attending training courses, involved on some other task within the school, etc. You may be brought in to do a special piece of work – organise something or provide support in some way. You may be in just one class the whole time or teach for an hour or two in every class in the school and all combinations in between. You may get plenty of notice or very little notice.
- Medium term – this can be from a couple of weeks to one or two terms and may start as a short contract and then be extended. Often you will not know in advance how long you will be in the post. This is usually with one class to cover a longer absence but may be covering 'McCrone time' or doing learning support, etc.
- Long term – this tends to be covering a maternity leave or long-term sickness or because there is the money or need for an extra member of staff but the school is not able to appoint a permanent member of staff. This may be for one or more years and might be to cover a teacher on secondment or to address a particular staffing issue. You will probably get more notice for this type of contract although it may still be that you have to simply turn up the following day.

Most LAs now have a pool of permanent supply teachers – these are permanent posts, advertised and interviewed for, and will be out of reach until you have obtained SFR. These teachers usually cover a number of schools and can be sent where needed. They are full-time posts and so will have roles in one or two schools that they take up when not needed for supply cover elsewhere. A Court of Session judgement affirmed that temporary teachers have a right to transfer to a permanent contract after a period of satisfactory full-time service, usually a minimum of two years, and many LAs are reviewing their staffing as a result of this (Menter et al., 2002). Currently the onus is on the teacher to request this.

Usually you will be contacted by the LA, who will advise you that there is work for you. You are not obliged to take every contract offered but would be wise to do so unless you have strong reasons for not wanting to work in a particular school or other reasons why you are unable to work at that time. You will be given details of the school and the type of contract and may be told which class you will be taking – details vary.

Check with the LA about the process of being paid for contracts. Usually, you will complete a form before leaving the school (short contracts) and the school will submit this to the LA with whom you will have already been registered and you will be paid through your bank account at the end of the month. You should always have your GTCS number and National Insurance number with you as you may require these to complete the form. The daily rate for supply teaching may be slightly different to the rate for a permanent class teacher because of adjustments made for holiday periods. Conditions of service vary between LAs and you should check when you register whether you will have an entitlement to CPD and holiday pay with that authority.

Preparation

Preparing to take up short contracts is different to working in a longer-term post.

Usually on a short contract you will have little notice and often not be familiar with the school or the class. The scenario may well involve you arriving in a class at about 10.0am in an unfamiliar school. You may need to find out, en route from the front door to the classroom:

- the name of the teacher you are replacing;
- times of breaks;
- location of assistance if you have problems – names of members of staff you can call on;
- any specific difficulties in the class, e.g. medical issues or children with particular problems;
- emergency exits and procedures;
- how you are expected to deal with toilet visits or bad behaviour;
- has any work been left for you?

The school may have a specially prepared booklet for you and you may have a chat with a member of the management team before you go into the classroom.

You may find yourself in a strange school, in a new classroom with up to 33 expectant faces all looking at you – preparation is the key to survival.

Firstly, you will not know where any of the everyday resources are so prepare a bag with some or all of the following.

- Stationery – pens, pencils, sharpeners, erasers, rulers, sticky tape, scissors, felt pens, highlighters, sticky notes, a pad of A4 paper – lined and plain, some plastic wallets, stapler. It can be difficult to find resources in someone else's room and you may not want to keep the class waiting while you hunt for a pair of scissors.
- Some instant activities, e.g. a number game of some sort; an alphabet game.
- Some worksheets suitable for that stage on general aspects of maths or language – perhaps a framework for a story or some maths problems or a general knowledge quiz. It is helpful to have a set photocopied already so that you won't need to find out about photocopying immediately, but make sure you photocopy a new set before you leave so that you have them ready for your next class.
- A story book suitable for the stage – try to choose a book of short stories that the children are not likely to have heard.
- Some resources for an afternoon activity – perhaps some unusual items like a set of plastic frogs that could be used as a prompt for some storytelling, drama, science, creative writing, art, etc.
- A couple of useful teachers' resource books that will give you good ideas.
- Resources for breaktime, e.g. a mug and teabags.

If you are travelling by car, it is helpful to have a box in the boot that has resources for various stages such as story books, some teacher's resource books – there are some excellent ones around – that will give you short topic ideas to occupy a couple of days. For example, a topic on 'Feet' might include measuring feet – length or area or comparing with height, a cut-out of an unusual footprint which could be used for creative writing or science, some assorted shoes for discussion and design, some foam to make footprint pads for art, etc. If you have some unusual items to use as a stimulus, e.g. an old camera or some old-style pennies, these could be in your box too. Try to reuse resources you have made as a student and keep those lessons in mind.

Have a list of lessons you can do quickly and with the minimum of resources – some language, maths, social studies, etc., with variations for different stages. Although there might be a plan left for the day, you might not find it practical to carry it all out – working on several different topics with four maths groups takes time to set up and you might need to have a whole-class lesson that you can do instead.

You should have everything ready to go and have either access to internet mapping or an A to Z with all the schools marked, so that if you get very short notice, you won't waste time trying to find it. Most LA websites have lists of primary schools – print them off so you can quickly find the address of the school in order to locate it.

Arriving in class

Once you have been left in the classroom, you must immediately assume control – don't stand dithering. You need to break the ice and if possible buy some time so that you can catch your breath, look around the room and identify the daily programme/diary, decide on your first activity, identify the helpful children (there are always one or two who can be relied on to tell you where the jotters are, etc.) and the challenging children – these will quickly become apparent.

Start straight away with an activity of some sort. If the children are already engaged on a task, return them to work, establishing firm control. Look quickly to find out what they are doing and if there is a diary or plan of work for the day. Don't try to immediately embark on group work – stick to some whole-class tasks. If there is a maths plan for example, put some assorted sums up on the board for everyone to do (preferably on some spare paper from your bag) while you have a look at textbooks and jotters and decide what to do next.

If the children are not engaged on a task, you need to set them to work doing something – making name cards is a useful start but have a novel idea for them to undertake and have the resources in your bag to do it. For example, they could make 'conference' name tags to put into plastic holders that you can buy from stationery shops (these are reusable for any number of classes) – they could draw themselves, give themselves a title or description, e.g., 'Helen Smith, Good at Writing and wearing a blue hairband'. Obviously the task needs to be adjusted for the stage you are teaching.

Look around the room once the children are engaged. Are there class rules on the wall? If there are, refer to them when explaining the behaviour you expect – do this regularly. If there is a daily plan, look through it and on some paper, make your own plan – what can you manage and what will you do of your own prepared activities?

In some situations, you will have been left a whole day's work already planned and resourced. This is a straightforward situation and you should be able to pick this up and work with it. There may be some things you are not comfortable teaching, e.g. if the lesson is on Egyptian gods, you might not have sufficient knowledge to teach it. Some things you will be able to pick up in a few minutes, others you will not. Insert one of your own activities in its place. Don't assume that you should teach some other aspect of the topic – this might upset the teacher's plan.

Ask reliable children if you need to find resources – there may be class monitors who will be a great help in handing things out and putting things away. When the bell goes for break, you might need directions to the staffroom.

The children are a great resource when it comes to class practice. How do they line up? Do they change their shoes? Where do they change for PE? – and usually they will delight in telling you the correct procedure. Take the day one step at a time – work out what you will do until lunch time then plan over lunch time for the afternoon.

Find out some more information about the routines at lunch time, particularly behaviour management or afternoon requirements, e.g. getting children out to a bus at home time.

Keep a firm hand on the behaviour – classes can often become livelier with a new teacher and you need to keep the lid on things. Remind the children of the class rules and nip any trouble in the bud quickly.

When you reach the end of the day

If you are not returning to the class tomorrow, tidy up and mark any work done in jotters – teachers get very upset when they return to unmarked work, and one day that will be you! Leave a note of what you have done during the day including details of work done from their daily plan and a brief note of any activities of your own. Any work from your own activities done on paper can be taken away unless it is particularly good or something the children will look for tomorrow. Remember to photocopy any sheets that you have used of your own to replace your stock. Get your contract form and your probationer form, if applicable, signed before you leave.

If you will be back the next day:

- Spend time with the weekly plan and any daily plans that have been left to see what is planned.
- Look in last week's diary and see what happened last week – it might be that for example PE or RME is following a sequence of lessons from a planner and you might be able to simply do the next lesson.
- Identify resources such as teaching packs, textbooks and workbooks that might be mentioned on the plans.
- If there are things you are not going to manage to teach or no plans left, plan the following day with your own lessons and gather resources as required.
- A member of the management team will probably pop in to see how you are doing – if you think of things to ask during the day, jot them down and write down the answers – there's a lot to take in.

An invaluable tool on short-term supply is a small file with alphabetical index dividers. Keep a record of all the teaching you do. Set up a page for each school you visit along the lines of the format below.

The first page will allow you to do some quick revision if you are called back to the school at a later date. It is good form to know names, etc. on a return visit and since there might be some time elapsing and possibly a number of other schools before you get called back, you should record as much as possible. The second page is a record of the teaching you did and the classes taught. If you have used one of your special lessons, you don't want to reappear in the same class six months later and try to repeat it.

Page 1

School	
Address	
Phone number	
Email address	
Head Teacher	
Depute/s	
Secretary	
Other Staff	
School Times	Morning – Afternoon –
Emergency	Fire –
School procedures	Behaviour scheme – Toilet visits – Photocopying – Resources –
Schemes of work	Maths – Reading – Science – PE – Others –
Notes	

Page 2

Record of teaching			
Date		Stage/Class teacher	Notes (including class procedures, lessons taught, etc.
Start	Finish		

If you are on a longer-term contract, then the above advice will be useful for your first day but you will have time to get to know the class and staff to some extent, depending how long you are there. If you are going into a class at the start of term then the advice given earlier in this chapter for the first day of TIS will apply.

You want to make a good impression wherever you go. Head teachers are often in contact with each other and the name of a good supply teacher may get passed around. There may be a job in that school in the future and you may want to try for it.

Some points to remember.

- You are in someone else's classroom – don't move things about, or at least put things back as they were before you leave.
- Don't use up special resources that you find in the class (e.g. rainbow paint) – it may have been bought in for a specific activity and not for general use.
- Don't touch someone else's wall display – if you need to put things up because you are there for a while, put a layer of paper over the current display and use reusable adhesive on this. When you leave the class, the whole sheet can be taken down to return the wall to normal (take advice on this if you are unsure).
- Behaviour management can be more difficult as a supply teacher and you may find that you get some of the more lively classes to teach, so you need to keep on top of this from the start – read up on strategies to use.
- Treat the classroom with respect – don't throw things out that are not of your making or tidy away things that you have not used.
- Return jotters to their proper places and don't take any away with you.
- The teacher will probably appreciate a brief description of work done while they have been away, but not a detailed essay.
- Your appearance in the class will often be a cause of light relief to the children – they may transfer their allegiance to you temporarily. Be professional and don't undermine the returning teacher with thoughtless comments.
- If you have been following a maths or language programme, leave a sheet giving details of the next lesson/unit/page numbers for each group.
- Remember to thank classroom assistants and staff for their help.
- Remember, you will probably be in the position of the returning teacher one day – do as you would be done by.

Applying for teaching posts

Towards the middle to end of your TIS or probationary period, you may start to apply for jobs as they begin to appear in the press for the next school year. This will affect your work in a number of ways:

- you will need time off for visits and interviews;
- you will want to use your probationary experience positively in your application;
- you will want to ask for references and ensure your referees are clear about what is required.

Time off for visits and interviews

Jobs are usually advertised by local authorities or in the case of independent schools by the school itself. When you respond to an advertisement the school or education authority will send you an information pack and details of how to apply for the job.

When you are considering applying for a job you may be invited to look around the school or you may ask to do so. This could present problems because of the time taken out of your current school, especially if you are applying for a job at some distance away. There is no doubt that an informal visit can be useful to you and some schools schedule specific times to take a large number of applicants around the school together. However, you must consider the impact of absence from school on your training. If you applied for six jobs, visited all the schools and went for interviews at each one, you would miss at least a week of work – two weeks if the schools you are applying to are not very close to your school. The school might have to employ a supply teacher to cover your absence so it may be better to try to visit schools after the end of the school day, or to explain to schools that your placement prevents you from visiting informally. You will almost always be given a tour of the school prior to interview and you would have the opportunity to withdraw from the interview after this is you did not think the school would suit you.

If you have applied for a post and are invited to interview, you should ask your head teacher for permission to attend: this will involve missing school that day or part of the day. In practice this is a courtesy and you will always be given permission to attend interviews. Mentors and head teachers will help you to prepare your application and you should discuss a draft of your letter of application, supporting statement or CV (whatever is requested) with your mentor, if possible. It is also a good idea to ask your mentor to help you to prepare for interview. Preparation might take a number of forms.

- Discussion of hot topics in the educational press or recent initiatives in school is always useful.
- Discussing these issues with your mentor will help you to explore the issues from another perspective. Consider what the effects of new ideas are for teachers, schools and children.
- Role-playing a mock interview with the mentor, teacher or another member of school staff can help you to conquer nerves and prepare your interview manner.

The interview procedure in Scotland does not usually include asking you to teach in class. However, if you are applying for a job in England, it is not uncommon. Ask your mentor to check your plans for teaching you are asked to do as part of your interview. Although you will not be able to prepare a perfect lesson because you do not know the children, you can still show that you know the relevant curricula, have good ideas, know a range of teaching strategies, are aware of a range of resources and have a good manner with the children. Your mentor may be able to spot obvious *faux pas* or overambitious plans if you ask to discuss them.

If you apply for a job in a local authority supply pool you will usually go for an interview for the pool which will be held usually in the council premises.

Using your probation experience in your application for a teaching post

You will probably be given support in applying for a teaching post as part of your LA CPD.

It is important that your application includes insights from your probation because this shows what you have learnt from your experiences.

When you write in response to an advertisement for a teaching post or for details of supply post, you will receive a specification for the job. This may be a set of general statements, like the sample below, or there may be very specific requirements associated with a school.

Sample teaching job specification

Experience
Appropriate teaching practice experience

Qualifications
SFR or the ability to achieve this before the job is due to start

Knowledge and skills
Knowledge and understanding of the curriculum requirements for the relevant age range.
Ability to plan, deliver, monitor and evaluate children's learning.
Knowledge and understanding of the principles of assessment and record-keeping and their use to promote the educational and personal development of the pupils.
Ability to communicate ideas clearly to a variety of groups.
Understanding of the requirements of children with special educational needs.
Ability to effectively manage and motivate children.
Ability to work as part of a team and to develop positive relationships with pupils, colleagues, parents and, where appropriate, outside agencies.
Ability to demonstrate a commitment to equality of opportunity for all pupils.
Ability to demonstrate a commitment to high educational standards and to maximising the achievement of all pupils.
Ability to demonstrate a commitment to continuing professional development.

There are two main types of written application for Primary and Early Years teaching posts:

- the LA application form, which usually includes a personal statement or letter of application;
- your own CV and letter of application.

The information pack you receive from the school or LA will tell you what is required.

Complete application forms neatly and accurately, in a way that will demonstrate enthusiasm. The usual rules for form-filling apply: read the instructions carefully and follow them. Write a draft first (and keep it for future reference); do not leave gaps – write N/A if appropriate; check all your dates and have all your information to hand; make sure your writing is neat and everything is correctly spelled and make sure your personal statement (or letter) is effective. Plan plenty of time to fill in your application – it takes longer than you think – and make sure you have done a thorough review of your placement and your record of professional development or training plan. If it is a local authority application form, it will probably be available online to be completed electronically then printed off to be posted. If it is not available from the LA website, contact human resources, who may be able to email it to you if this is your preferred method of completion.

You may be required to write either a supporting statement or letter of application as part of the form or a supporting letter. The first thing you should do to prepare this is to examine thoroughly the specification and/or job description to work out what the school or LA is looking for. Then read the instructions for completing the form very carefully. Filling out this form is a chore but it is your chance to market your skills. Do not be too modest or make exaggerated claims. You may find the completed form slightly embarrassing, because it spells out your achievements and qualities, but it should not be untruthful.

There are many ways of writing your letter of application or supporting statement but the following points should be considered.

- Say why you are applying for this post in particular. Include any local links, faith issues or visits to the school.
- Give a brief overview of your training (but do not repeat everything you have put in the application form). Also mention your degree (PGDE) and any relevant projects or experiences.
- Reference to your probation placement including:
  - where you are completing your TIS;
  - when you expect to complete it;
  - the class you have been teaching.
- You may also include details of student placements –
  - where and when you did the placement;
  - what stages you have taught;
  - the level of responsibility you took.
- Special features of the placement such as open-plan schools or team teaching.
- Examples of how you plan, teach, monitor and evaluate learning outcomes, behaviour management strategies, work with parents, etc.
- Write a little about your vision or beliefs for primary education and the principles that underpin your practice. This might be how children learn, classroom management, teaching styles, etc. This gives the school a flavour of what you are like as a teacher.
- Details of your personal experiences; leisure interests or involvement with children. Make these relevant to your work as a teacher.

One of the easier ways to organise this information is to identify a number of subheadings taken from the specification or job description, such as:

- teaching experience;
- commitment to teaching;
- knowledge, skills and aptitudes;
- planning and organisation;
- strengths and interests;
- personal qualities.

Organise your information under these headings. You can then remove your subheadings and have a well-organised letter to discuss with your mentor.

PRACTICAL TASK PRACTICAL TASK PRACTICAL TASK PRACTICAL TASK PRACTICAL TASK

Use the specification above to review your experience, qualifications and knowledge, skills and aptitudes. Go through each point, asking yourself:

What evidence do I have that I meet this criterion?

What have I learned about this on my placement?

What else do I need to be able to do to achieve this?

Finally, ask yourself what you want to focus on in your continuing professional development during the next year.

Write a letter of application, of not more than two sides of A4, setting out your experience, knowledge, skills and aptitudes and views about education. Discuss this general draft with your mentor and ask her to tell you about the impact and the impression it makes.

Preparing a CV

You may find yourself writing a *curriculum vitae* (CV) for the first time for a job application. Your CV sets out the important information about you, usually on no more than two sides of A4. Make sure you have some good-quality, white paper to print on.

If you are basing your CV on a version you have used before, do not just churn it out for job after job. Check first that it matches the specification for each individual job.

Things you can leave out of a CV

There is no need to include your date of birth, age, marital status or ethnic origin.

- A photograph is not necessary for teaching CVs and can trigger subconscious prejudice.
- Do not include your reasons for changing jobs. Keep your CV factual: where you worked and when.
- Do not include failures on your CV. Keep it focused on what you have achieved.
- Do not include salary information.

Things to include on your CV

- Contact details. Make sure that contact details you give will really reach you: if you have an email address that you rarely check, do not include it. Ideally, include your postal address, any telephone numbers you have (landline and mobile) and your email address if you will be checking it frequently.
- Your gender, if it is not obvious from your name.
- A short skills summary or supporting statement (see below).
- Your education. This is best organised as follows: primary, secondary, further, higher.
- Your qualifications, listed with the most recent first, including results.
- Your work experience and placement experiences – most recent first (any positions you held more than about ten years ago can be left out).
- Interests – only real and genuine ones, e.g. any sports you actively participate in. If these hobbies and interests can convey a sense of your personality, all the better. Include any non-teaching qualifications that may have arisen from your hobbies or interests here as well.
- Membership of professional associations (not unions).
- Nationality, National Insurance number and referee details (or a sentence to say, 'Referees available on request') can be included at the end of your CV.

A skills summary need only be around 200 words, but you can still cover a lot of ground.

- Write in the first person.
- Every word must be relevant and grammar should be immaculate.
- Use interesting adverbs and adjectives to lift the text.
- Do not just focus on experience. Achievements, accountability and competence are more important.

- Aim to give a sense of your creativity, personal management and integrity: the reader will want to see that you have strong communication skills and are perhaps even leadership material.
- Some people prefer to include a short bulleted list of around six key skills.

Suggested layout

- When designing your CV, you need to be economical with space. While the page should not look cluttered, excess space will look messy and ill thought-out.
- Present your contact details across the top of the first page (like a letterhead) to preserve space.
- Use a clear, standard font such as Times New Roman or Arial.
- Avoid abbreviations unless they are universally understood.
- If you really cannot fit everything on to two sides of A4, try reducing the font size slightly. This will mean the print is still large enough to read, but will give you a little more room to play with. Avoid lines of just one or two words, as this is a waste of space.
- When you have designed your CV on screen, print a draft version and try to view it through fresh eyes. Is it likely to grab the attention of a reader within a few seconds? Is it visually pleasing? Are there any errors? It is a good idea to ask someone else to cast an eye over it as it is easy to miss typographical errors on documents you have been working on yourself.
- Be aware that this is not a one-off task. Once you have completed your CV, you will need to keep it up to date.

A sample CV

Emily Jones
21 Sandhills Drive, Brookfarm, Fife
Telephone: 0128 678 3567, mobile: 07887 987654, email: *EMMY00@aol.com*

I am just completing my induction year in a ... primary school. My previous work experience as an accountant in Glasgow enabled me to develop an understanding of management in a large multinational corporation as well as demonstrable communication skills. Part of my role was the delivery of internal training for new staff. During my initial teacher training I taught in an inner-city nursery and a primary school with a large multi-racial population. In addition to my teaching I developed a successful after-school science club which was open to all children in P6 and involved their parents in a final presentation of the science they had learned.

Education
Primary: 1982–1988 Brookfarm Primary School, Fife
Secondary: 1988–1995 Merchiston High School, Dunfermline
Higher: 1995–1998 University of Warwick BA
1998–2004 Membership of the Society of Chartered Accountants
2004–2005 Faculty of Education, Strathclyde University, PGDE

Qualifications
PGDE: Primary Education
Degree: mathematics and statistics 2.1
Higher: mathematics A; statistics A; physics B; English B; French C.
Standard Grades: mathematics A, English A, chemistry B, physics B, history A, ICT A, art B, geography B, French A, biology B

Professional development
During my initial teacher training I completed an LA-run First Aid in the Classroom course and attended a 'Developing Storysacks' training day.

Work experience
2002–2003 ITE placements: Grove School Nursery, West Primary School, Glasgow
1998–2002 British International Bank, London, Accountant
1995–1998 Vacation positions with Marks and Spencer and Waterstones, Glasgow

Interests
I have run a local Brownies group for some years. I also run to keep fit and have completed the Glasgow and London marathons.

Additional qualifications
Full, clean driving licence.
Strathclyde Junior Football Coaching

Nationality
British

National Insurance Number
TY123456B

Referees available on request

Asking for references

You will usually be asked to supply the names, positions and contact details of two referees. The first should be the head teacher or your mentor in your school. If you do not get a first reference from your school, the job advertiser will usually assume you have something to hide.

Refer to the notes on the application to see who they require for the second reference. It might ask for a senior member of staff of your university. Check carefully who this should be. It is common for universities to use the name of the head of department, even though your tutor will write the reference. It is essential to get this name right since the reference system in a large ITE provider will be geared up to a swift response but it will only work if you get the right name. The wrong name will slow down your reference and may put you at a disadvantage. The notes might suggest someone else who knows you very well or with whom you have taught.

Interview portfolios

As part of your probation, you will be maintaining your portfolio to demonstrate your achievement of the standards. This will contain assessment reports, observation feedback, mentor meeting notes and evidence of CPD and attainment.

You may be asked to take this training plan or record with you to interview. Even if you are not asked to bring a portfolio you may want to do so. You can offer this to your interviewers

– they do not have to spend much time looking at it but it does indicate you are well prepared and professional.

An interview portfolio can be a substantial document but, more usually, is a slim document containing some of the following:

- title and content page, preferably with a photo of you teaching happily on it;
- concise CV;
- interim report;
- a really good lesson plan or two, some examples of the work associated with the lesson and the lesson evaluation;
- a mentor observation of a lesson;
- a sample mentor meeting summary;
- an example of a written piece of work (and the marking sheet) if relevant;
- a few photos of you teaching. Choose these carefully as you really want to present a specific image. Generally you might choose one photo of you teaching a large group or class, one of you looking sensitive with a group and, ideally, one of you teaching elsewhere – pond-dipping is ideal. Remember, choose photos to suit a particular job. If the school is very ICT conscious, make sure there is a picture with you using ICT. If the school is keen to improve its physical education, a photo of your tag rugby lesson would be ideal. Make sure you follow your placement school's policy on photograph use and that the school and children are not identifiable;
- one or two photographs of displays, school visits you have been on, after school clubs or assemblies you have done;
- any evidence of your special interest – coaching certificates, first aid, cookery, etc.

In practice, trainees tell us that interview panels do not spend much time on interview portfolios and usually just flick through the content. However, by preparing this you not only demonstrate professionalism but also have the chance to present a tailored image of your achievements to the panel in addition to your written application.

Resources

Draper J. and O'Brien J., (2006) *Induction – Fostering Career Development at all Stages*. Edinburgh: Dunedin Academic Press.

The GTCS has a whole section of its website devoted to probationary teachers – www.gtcs.org.uk/probationweb/ Here you can find all sorts of help and advice, hints and tips from newly qualified teachers as well as a blog to share your experiences with others in the same position – particularly useful if you are the only probationer in the school.

Canter L., and Canter M. (2001) *Assertive Discipline: Positive Behaviour Management for Today's Classroom*. Sacramento: Canter and Associates.

Menter, I., Holligan, C., Hutchings, M. and Seagraves, L., Dalgety, J. (2002) *Insight 12 – The Management of Supply Cover in the Teaching Profession – SEED*. A report on Supply Teaching including aspects of pay, terms and conditions can be found at www.scotland.gov.uk/Publications/2004/01/18749/31631

The National CPD team have produced advice and guidance on CPD for supply teachers. It can be found at www.ltscotland.org.uk/cpdscotland/images/OP7v2_tcm4-397912.pdf

Most school vacancies are advertised in the *Times Educational Supplement Scotland* (Fridays)
www.tesjobs.co.uk

The Guardian (Tuesdays)
www.jobsunlimited.co.uk

The Daily Telegraph (Independent Schools)
www.telegraph.co.uk

The Independent (Thursdays)
www.independent.co.uk

Some of these operate an electronic job alert system.

For general information about teaching in the private sector:
Independent Schools Council Information Service (ISCIS) at www.iscis.uk.net

Incorporated Association of Preparatory Schools (IAPS) at www.iaps.co.uk

Your union is an excellent source of help, advice and support in applying for a teaching post:
www.askatl.org.uk (ATL)
www.eis.org.uk (EIS)
www.teachersunion.org.uk (NASUWT)
www.data.teachers.org.uk (NUT)

Other useful online resources for finding a teaching post are available at:
www.eteach.com
www.teachernet.gov.uk
www.prospects.ac.uk

Make sure you use you local or university careers service.

The UKSchoolGuide.com website is a directory of all schools based in the UK, and is the first online guide to celebrate the successes and achievements of schools throughout the UK. It is a useful resource for schools to promote themselves and is completely free. It will help prospective teachers find out more about schools to which they wish to apply for teaching positions.

Visit www.ukschoolguide.com

Glossary

5–14 curriculum The curriculum for Scotland which was introduced in 1991 and reviewed in 2000. It is currently the curriculum in use but is in the process of being replaced by the Curriculum for Excellence.

AoL Assessment of Learning see Summative Assessment.

ASL Additional Support for Learning children who require additional support for whatever reason long or short term. The term was coined in the Education (Additional Support for Learning) (ASL) (Scotland) Act 2004. It replaces the term 'special educational needs' which was limited in application to children who had learning difficulties. The new term includes any children who need extra support.

Assessment is for Learning The Scottish government programme to introduce formative assessment in schools.

ATL Association of Teachers and Lecturers. For further details see www.askatl.org.uk/

BEd Bachelor of education degree can be completed with teaching to achieve the Standard for Initial Teacher Education (SITE). If completed without teaching it is simply a degree in education.

CA Classroom assistant – someone who is employed to work in a support role within the school. They might have a range of qualifications from none to degree standard since this role is sometimes taken by graduates wishing to gain classroom experience in order to gain a place on a PGDE course to become a teacher. They might work within a number of classes at specified times or have a more general role within the school. As a class teacher you will be expected to provide a role for them when they are with you either in a teaching support role or in preparation of materials, etc.

Class teacher The teacher responsible for a particular class. This role might be shared between two teachers, called a 'job-share', who will work together but will usually not be in the class at the same time. A number of other teachers may teach the class at various times but the class teacher has overall responsibility.

Curriculum for Excellence (ACfE) The new curriculum currently being produced by LTS which addresses education from ages 3 to 18.

Curriculum Framework 3–5 The curriculum for children aged between 3 and 5 years old. Currently under review (see Curriculum for Excellence).

CPD Continuing professional development. For further details see www.teachernet/gov/uk/professionaldevelopment/

DfES Department for Education and Skills. The English government department which creates policy. For further details see www.dfes.gov.uk/

Disclosure The process by which anyone who wants to work with children is checked against the criminal records through the Criminal Records Bureau (CRB) or the Scottish Criminal Record Office Disclosure Service.

EAL English as an additional language – children who are do not have English as their first language learn English as an additional language.

Early Years education Education provided for children aged from birth up to primary school age at around 5 years. Usually for teacher education, the term is used for education from 4 to 5 years and usually takes place in a nursery school or class.

Extended school A school that provides a range of services and activities often beyond the school day to help meet the needs of its pupils, their families and the wider community. For more information see www.qca.org.uk/10013.html

Formative assessment Assessment that is carried out throughout the teaching to monitor understanding and achievement. The essential factor is to modify the teaching as a result of what is learned from the assessment. It includes strategies such as stating clearly what you intend the children to learn – WALT (We are learning to …) so that they understand the focus of the lesson, and explaining what your assessment will be based on WILF (What I'm looking for…).

Foundation Stage The earliest years of schooling for UK children (ages 3–5 years) used in England, Wales and Northern Ireland. For more information see www.qca.org.uk/160.html

Four capacities The characteristics described in ACfE which the curriculum and schools should be aiming to develop in pupils (see Curriculum for Excellence).
- successful learners;
- confident individuals;
- responsible citizens;
- effective contributors.

Gaelic medium Teaching that is delivered wholly or partly in Gaelic.

GTCE General Teaching Council for England and GTCW General Teaching Council for Wales. The GTC is the professional body for teaching in England and Wales whose purpose is to help improve standards of teaching and the quality of learning in the public interest. www.gtce.org.uk or www.gtcw.org.uk

GTCS General Teaching Council for Scotland the regulatory body for teaching in Scotland.

HEI Higher education institution – a university, school or college offering degree-level and postgraduate education.

HMIE Her Majesty's Inspectorate for Education the body that is responsible for inspecting and maintaining standards in Scottish schools.

Humanities A collective term for a range of subjects including: history, geography, religious studies, sociology and others.

ICT Information and communications technology. For more information see www.becta.org.uk/

IEP Individualised Education Plan – a programme of learning that is devised to respond to the particular needs of a child.

Independent schools These are schools that are not funded by the government.

Induction period See Probationary period.

Inset In-service education and training. Training for qualified teachers.

ITE Initial Teacher Education the course of training that must be completed successfully before a student can become a probationary teacher

ITT Initial teacher training. Course of training that leads to qualified teacher status (QTS) in England, Wales and Northern Ireland. For further information see www.tda.gov/uk/

ITT provider A university that offers initial teacher training courses. For more information see www.tda.gov/uk/partners/funding/accreditation/ittproviders.aspx

IWB Interactive whiteboard a whiteboard which is electronically linked to a computer and has a touch-sensitive surface that allows interaction with the computer through a special pen or with the hand or finger, depending on the type.

Key Stages The different stages of compulsory schooling in England, Wales and Northern Ireland.

Foundation Key Stage Children aged 3–5 or EYFS Children aged birth to 5.

LA Local authority.

Learning outcomes Sometimes called Learning Objectives the intended result of a lesson what you intend the children to learn.

Learning Support Teacher A teacher whose role is to provide specialist support for learning within the school.

LSA Learning support assistant.

LTS Learning and Teaching Scotland the government-funded body that provides information and support for teachers across Scotland.

Maintained school A school that is maintained by the state.

Mentor supporter The person in school who manages your placement offering advice, support and, usually, assessing your progress. The details of the role of your mentor will be in your course information.

MFL Modern foreign languages. French, Spanish, German, Gujarati, etc. The government is committed to introducing MFL for all primary pupils by 2010. For further details see www.qca.org.uk/10076_10943.html

NASUWT National Union of Schoolmasters Union of Women Teachers. For further details see www.nasuwt.org.uk/

National Assessment/Testing The programme by which children are tested in maths, reading and writing when the teacher is satisfied that they have achieved the next level within the 5–14 curriculum.

National Priorities for Education A set of five areas set by the government for educationalists to use as a focus when engaged in self-evaluation.

NC National Curriculum for England, Wales and Northern Ireland. Covers what pupils should be taught in state-maintained schools. The National Curriculum embraces 12 subjects overall, and is divided into four Key Stages according to age. Available online at www.curriculumonline.gov.uk/

Non-denominational school A school that is not linked to a religious institution.

NQT Newly qualified teacher. A teacher in England, Wales and Northern Ireland who has just been recommended for qualified teacher status and who needs to complete an induction period to confirm the award. For more information see www.tda.gov.uk/teachers/induction.aspx

NUT National Union of Teachers. For more information, see www.teachers.org.uk/

Ofsted Office for Standards in Education. The body responsible for inspection in England, Wales and Northern Ireland in schools and teacher training. See www.ofsted.gov.uk/

OTTP Overseas trained teacher programme. An individually tailored programme of training and assessment enabling OTTs to achieve qualified teacher status in England. For more information, see www.tda.gov/uk/Recruit/thetrainingprocess/typesofcourse/ottp.aspx

P1, P2, etc. Primary 1 the first class in a primary school, Primary 2 the second class in a primary school, etc.

PE Physical education.

PGDE Post Graduate Diploma in Education one-year training course for graduates allowing them to achieve the Standard for Initial Teacher Education.

PLP Personal Learning Plan an assessment carried out by children, with the support of their teacher, in which they set out their own targets and achievements.

Pre-5 A term often used to describe education of children up to the age of 5.

Primary education The education provided for children aged 5 to 12 years.

Probationary period Time spent after completing ITE, when the teacher is partly qualified but still training while practising to achieve the final standard as a teacher. Otherwise known as induction.

Profile This is the document completed at the end of your ITE which sets out your progress towards meeting the Standards for ITE and your targets for future work. It may have another name (report, assessment ,etc.). It will form part of your training record.

Provisional registration The first level of registration with the GTCS on completion of ITE that allows a student to work as a probationary teacher.

PSHE Personal, social and health education.

PTA Parent-teacher association. For general information see www.ncpta.org.uk/

QCA Qualifications and Curriculum Authority. See www.qca.org.uk/

QTS Qualified Teacher Status. The status trainee teachers achieve in England, Wales and Northern Ireland; recommendation for this by meeting all of the required Standards. It is confirmed after a period of induction. You must have this qualification to teach in a state-maintained school. For more information, see www.tda.gov.uk/Recruit/becomingateacher/qualifiedteacherstatus.aspx

Schools in special measures Schools deemed by Her Majesty's Chief Inspector of Schools to be failing to provide an acceptable standard of education for its pupils.

Scottish Executive See Scottish government.

Scottish government The devolved government for Scotland was known as the Scottish Executive when it was formed in 1999 but from 2007 was renamed the Scottish government.

Scottish Qualifications Authority National body in Scotland responsible for the development, accreditation, assessment, and certification of qualifications other than degrees.

SEN Special Education Needs see ASL.

SENCO SEN co-ordinator. The teacher in school with responsibility for the delivery of services for children with special educational needs.

Setting The arrangement whereby children are re-arranged into ability groupings across a number of classes for specific curricular areas usually maths and language.

SFR Standard for Full Registration the standard that must be reached to become a fully qualified teacher.

SITE Standard for Initial Teacher Education the standard that must be reached to successfully complete the first stage of teacher training undertaken partly in university and partly in school.

Summative assessment Assessment which is carried out at the end of a piece of work to assess achievement, e.g. class test.

Supply teaching A contract with a local authority that allows you to teach where needed on a short- to long-term basis. Used to cover teacher absences or particular short-term needs for extra teaching staff.

TES *Times Educational Supplement*. A good source of information about teaching job vacancies in England, Wales and Northern Ireland. See www.tes.co.uk/

TESS *Times Educational Supplement Scotland*. A good source of information about teaching job vacancies. See www.tes.co.uk/

TIS Teacher Induction Scheme the one-year supported post in school that is sponsored by the government to enable provisional teachers to complete their probation.

Transition The movement from one establishment to another usually refers to the move from nursery to primary school or from primary to secondary school.

Voluntary aided schools Schools in England and Wales, maintained by the LEA, for which a foundation (generally religious) appoints most of the governing body.

Voluntary controlled schools Schools in England and Wales, maintained by the LEA, for which a foundation (generally religious) appoints some – but not most – of the governing body.

WALT We are Learning To ... see Formative assessment

WILF What I am Looking For ... see Formative assessment